VORWERK
TIP OF THE WEEK

The Ultimate Handbook
to Become a Successful Dance Music Producer

Quote

"Making a hit is easier then getting paid for it"

– M.Vorwerk

ISBN: 978-1-54390-270-9 (print)
ISBN: 978-1-54390-271-6 (ebook)

CONTENTS

Background story

Hi Producers and welcome to my studio.

My name is Maarten Vorwerk, I live in Aruba but I was born in The Netherlands.

I started producing Electronic music back in 1996.

At first I was producing Dutch hardcore music, then made my way into Trance, followed on into Jump/Hardstyle and after that I started making Commercial Club/Pop Music.

In 2001 I finished my degree at the SAE (school of audio engineering)

I see myself as a producer with a very broad set of producing skills instead of a producer being really good in one particular style.

At the start of my producing career I was working at a recordcompany. During the daytime I was picking orders for cd and vinyl shops across the world. I always had my hands on the latest releases and by the amount they were leaving the warehouse I could clearly tell what was working on the dancefloor and what was not.

At night I used that knowledge to my advantage and started producing every day after work until midnight. Sleeping was never an option. And I committed all my time to this.

Finally I got good enough to start releasing tracks for the recordcompany I worked for. Which was pretty cool cause I was able to sell and pack my own cd's and vinyls. In 2005 I got the opportunity to work fulltime in the studio at that same recordcompany. From thereon out I really started building out my career. I produced a great amount of tracks under a lot of different aliases. Most of them became vinyl and cd-single releases and some tracks just winded up on the compilation cd's the recordcompany put out. In 2006 I scored the first big hit in Holland under my alias 'Jeckyll & Hyde'. The track 'Frozen Flame' ended up in the top ten of the Dutch top 40 and paved the way for the followup single 'Freefall' which reached the coveted number one spot and became one of the most sold singles in Holland in 2007. It started a massive dance hype in Holland and big parts of Europe, called 'Jumpstyle'. I won several awards, including the TMF award (dutch mtv).

In 2009 the recordcompany closed his doors. Severe mismanagement and not figuring out the digital side of business quick enough caused them to go bankrupt.

That was the time I started out for myself. I rented an office and build two studios in them.

The musicindustry was changing at a rapid pace and vinyls and cd's disappeared from the market. At that time I struggled quite a bit. I got approached to do some production work for another DJ, which I gladly took on. I started to produce more and more for other DJ's and it didn't take long for the word to get out. I stopped releasing music under my own aliases and decided to fully focus on 'Ghost Producing'. Between 2009 and 2014 I produced a lot of tracks. I combined the harder Dutch genres with more clubmusic and pulled the bpm back to 128 instead of 140-150.

This was the time when the Bigroom sound evolved to its current popular genre.

In 2011 the second number one hit in Holland was a fact with the track "Epic by Quintino & Sandro Silva". Both of the number one tracks were instrumentals, which is a one-of-a-kind achievement. In that timeframe I scored several top ten hits under many different names and was really helping to boost DJ careers.

Because I was always producing for other people and in the background it gave me an unique perspective on the music industry.

In 2014 I decided to leave everything behind in Holland and start over again in Aruba.

So I moved with my girl to Aruba and continued my production work over there.

#Vorwerk #TipOfTheWeek

In March 2014 I started my weekly blog on Facebook.

The #Vorwerk #TipOfTheWeek series.

With these tips I want to provide everybody the knowledge they need to become a better producer and give them a better view of the music industry.

My path was far from easy and if I knew then what I know now then it would have saved me a lot of headaches.

Back when I started producing we didn't have Youtube or the internet to look up theory or practical tips. So most of the stuff, I learned from trial and error, life lessons and some from books.

For the last three years I've written down 156 Tips and bundled them all together in this book.

All the tips in here are meant to help you underway. To form your mind-set towards your own practical approach. To improve your mixing skills, to see different approaches for the same problem, to make you a better producer and to make you aware of some of the business things you should know.

While producing and mixing you tend to forget some of the tricks over time and by having this book in your studio it will keep you sharp and inventive to keep trying out new things.

So it doesn't matter if you are a beginner or a seasoned veteran, this will be your ultimate handbook.

If you like to follow my future #Vorwerk #TipOfTheWeeks you can visit my facebook page at: www.facebook.com/vorwerkmaarten

TIP 1

Sidechain Effect

Try to sidechain a gate on your lead sound to get more control on the tail of your sound.

Keep your attack short and start playing around with the release of the gate. You will notice that the tails of the reverb will be cut off nicely without loosing the reverb feel. This will prevent your mix from clogging up.

TIP 2

Subboom Effect

Take a sub kick. Stretch it by half the tempo, 4 times over.
Add a down pitchbend. There's your subboom.

Reverse it to get a low sweep riser type effect. Adjust the sound with filters, EQ's and fade-ins to your liking.

TIP 3

Reverb & Delays

If you use reverbs & delay.
Try to make 2 or 3 good ones and only use those for your track
Try to mute the effects from your vst synthesizers.
This will make the track less blurry.

TIP 4

Loudness

When mixing a track to a certain loudness.
Take a track you like, set your volume knob/fader to a fixed point. Remember how loud that track sounded and try to mix your track towards it. In my case I know how loud a track should sound when my volume knob is at 10 o'clock. Mixing towards that is a different story but it is a great guideline.

TIP 5

Left and Right EQ

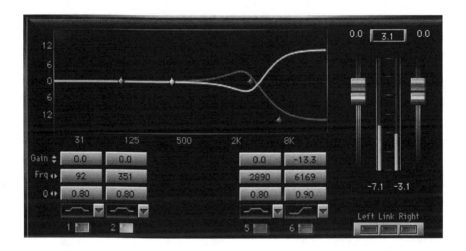

Many Eq vst's allow you to give the
L and R channel seperate eq.
This done right it widens up your sound.

TIP 6

Multiband Compressor

Try to misuse a multiband compressor as an equalizer on your lead sound and discover what happens!

TIP 7

Presence

If you want to create more presence on a sound. Put a reverb on it with a short pre-delay and short reverb time.

This will definitely bring your sound more upfront.

TIP 8

EQ'ing

When EQ'ing sounds. It's more important how they sound in the mix then solo'd.
Cut out all the frequencies you don't want to hear.
Even if you don't hear them.
You could use a spectrum analyzer for a visual reference.

TIP 9

How to create more attack on your Kicks

Find the kick you want to work with. Make sure you have it at the right volume. Now if you feel that the attack of the kick isn't punching thru enough

Then there is an alternative technique you could use instead of compression. You pull out a reference track which you like and then you are going to sample only the attack part of a kick you hear in that track. That would be a sample of only a few milliseconds since it's only the attack part of a kick. After that you put that on top of the original kick, you cut out the low-end and you mix it in gently until you feel that the kick punches thru enough.

Attack gives more tok
Decay gives more presence
Sustain & Release gives more low-end and a longer tail

TIP 10

Motivation

Making music is like cooking.
It's all about the chef and not the kitchen.
No matter where you live or how poor you are.
It's still posible to make that one hit in your bedroom.
All you need is a good idea, which will define you,
Make you stand out against others.
The rest will follow automatically!

TIP 11

Louder = Wider

If you want a louder mix you have to make your mix sound wider. U could use for instance

- panning
- enhancing
- delays
- reverb

This will make sure that there is still room for all elements in the track. It also creates a bit more headroom and more possibilities to increase the sound level.

TIP 12

Hard Disk Clipping

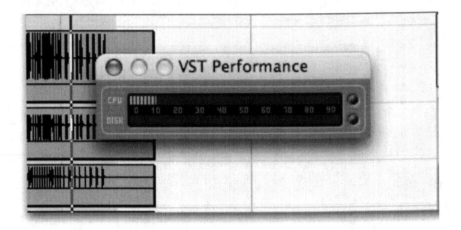

If you experience hard disk clipping during your production process.
Make an archive of your audio samples in your project folder.
This is an option most DAW's have.
After that it's gone!

TIP 13

Mixing Vocals

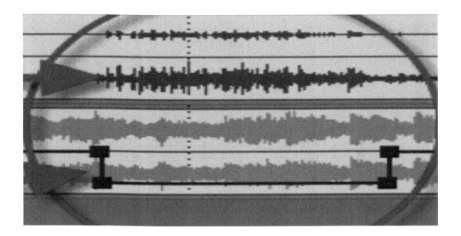

When mixing vocals on top of a drop make sure you duck the volume of the lead synths a couple dB on where the vocal is. This way the vocal will always stand out even in the busiest parts of the track.

TIP 14

Stereo Imaging

This is an unconventional tip.

Bounce your finished lead to audio. Duplicate the track.

Filter all the low frequencies (at least everything under 500 Hz) of the duplicated lead.

Put a stereo enhancer with a touch of hall verb on it. And take the volume fader down.

Now gently mix it back in until you feel you have made a wider lead sound.

Kick vs Basline

If you make a bass line orientated track you should use a shorter kick drum. So there is more room for the bass. You don't necessarily need to cut off the low from the kick since it's short anyway. But the kick works better when it has more 'tok' 80-120hz.

Then after you added your bass line and mixed it in with whatever you use (compressors, eq, gate, sidechain etc.) and you are still not happy with the low end. Then you could cut every thing below 50 or 60 hz on that bassline and add a little altered sinewave

Underneath it with the same midi pattern and put a lowpassfilter on the sinewave to only keep the lowend. This usually sounds a lot tighter and warmer!

TIP 16

Layering Synths

Depending on if it's necessary to layer synths you can use this as a good starting principle.

Three layers:

- low frequency bass layer: give those the same Att, Dec, Rel as the main synth. So they are in close sync. frequencies between 50 Hz - 500 Hz
- main synth: the synth which you think gives power to the break or drop. frequencies between 500 Hz - 5kHz.
- character sound: a sound in the high freq area which will give you lead that bit of extra character. Could be anything from a piano to a church bell 5kHz and higher.

Make sure you have volume control over these three layers and blend them together until you received a warm powerful sound.

TIP 17

Cool Effect

This works best on a vocal but you can use this on everything.
Take a piece of an audio sample.
Reverse the sample (so it plays backwards). Then apply some long tail reverb on it. Render it. And then Reverse it back again.
Great for introducing break melodies or start offs for vocals.

TIP 18

Taking control of your mixdown

When your mix is getting a bit 'messy' it is a good thing to reroute your tracks to several groups.

Try to keep things organised and divide your mix for instance into;

- Kick
- Beats
- Bass
- Leads
- FX
- Vocals.

This way you will regain easy control over your volume settings (among other things) before entering the final mixbus.

TIP 19

Mid-Side EQ - Stereo widening - Mastering.

Some EQ vst's have the function Mid-Side. (Fabfilter Pro-Q, Ozone, Voxengo, etc..). The Mid channel is the center of a stereo image. When the Mid channel is boosted, the listener perceives a more centered (mono) sound to the audio.

The Side channels are the edges of a stereo image. When the Side channel is boosted, the listener perceives a more spacious (wider) sound to the audio.

This way you can Equalize the mid and the side from the same signal seperately.

You can for instance boost the high frequencies on the side info. This will give a bit wider sound.

It's also easier to cutoff low frequencies from The Side while maintaining the ones from the mid. This way you create more mid focus on the low end of that signal.

You can use this technique really good while mastering or when creating layered synths.

Try to compare normal EQ with Mid-Side EQ and hear the difference.

TIP 20

Bussiness tip

Today a very short message, but one of the most important things you can learn:

Do business with common sense
And make music with compassion
Never mix one with the other!

TIP 21

Vocal Mixing

Vocal Mixing is something I don't like .
However there is a basic that I often use.

- Compression

Use a bit of compression to even out the volume of the track.
So the loudest peaks of the vocal are more under control and the softest
parts of the vocal are being brought up to a higher volume
For instance with the fabfilter Pro C you can see the amount of compression and how the peaks are compressed which can be very handy.

- Reverb

Use a reverb with a pre-delay which matches the bpm of your track. U use
a pre-delay to make sure the vocal doesn't drown in your mix.
To calculate the right pre-delay you can use this formula:
60000 divided by the bpm. For a 128 bpm track that would be 469ms for a
quarter note. But I prefer the 16th Note (=117ms)

- Delay settings

You can use the same formula to calculate the delay time (or use a sync
button). Usually a 1/4 note delay gives a nice flow. Make sure you don't
put the feedback to high.

- Eq

Eq to taste. Body of a vocal normally lies between 200-500 Hz.

But everybody else uses their own insert chain.
Everything below 80Hz you can cut away.

Parallel Compression

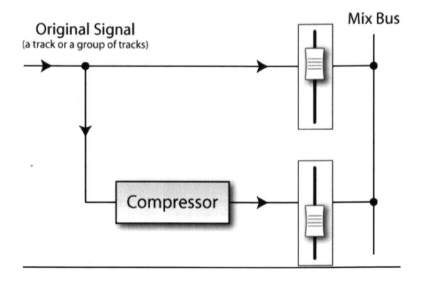

The basics of Parallel compression:

When you want to make a sound/vocal or a group or a whole track sound fatter you can use a trick called parallel compression.

The idea behind it is that you keep the dynamics of the higher volume peaks but you heavily compress the low volumes of the sound.

How to do this.
Mix a dry signal and leave it untouched and send that signal to a bus which you heavily compress. Use short attack times and long release times with a deep threshold (but play around to see what fits best). A long release time will make sure that the bus signal will be as 'flat' compressed as possible.
After that you mix some of the compressed signal back into the mixdown until it creates a fatter sound without harming the dynamics to much.

If you get phasing issues. Use time delay compensation or put the same compressor on the dry signal without any effective settings.

Key Of A Track

How to pick a key of a track?

Now I don't have any musical knowledge regarding notes and stuff.
But I normally base the key of the track on what goal you want to achieve
with the track.

Now this is based on my opinion but this is how I differentiate in general sense:

G = I've think that this key carries the most energy for cool/tough tracks
F = Also cool but you can give the low end a bit more low.
E = For really Low kick based tracks
A = For more emotional melodies and stuff.
C,D and B = more for commercial happy stuff.

The key in minor makes it a bit more sadder and darker. The key in major
a bit more happy and open .

Kick enhancement

Today I have a very special tip which you can use to enhance your Bigroom Kick.
It's a very difficult one, so pay close attention and keep on trying until it sounds right for your project/drop.

So you have made your bigroom kick which last a full quarter note.
This kick is of course in a certain key.
Now find a cool gritty bass sound and put it on top of the kick in the same key. Also for a full quarter note. Make sure the bass sound rolls a bit of using an lfo-pitch assigning.

Now they probably don't sound very well on top of each other.
Your bigroom kick has already got enough low-end. So start with cutting off the low end on the gritty bassline.

After this put a reversed sidechain on top of your kick. So that it starts hard and then rolls of. This will make your kick a bit tighter and shorter.

Then put a normal Sidechain on the gritty bassline.

Try to mix the crossover points of the 2 sidechains to each other so that the kick will sound as a whole.
Keep tweaking those crossover points and the low frequencies of the bas sound until it sounds right and they don't conflict with each other.

If this isn't enough of an enhancement then you can also add some "vocal riding" on the afterbeat (Manual, no plugin!) to your gritty bassline to give it a bit more dynamic feel and swing. Experiment with this, it's fun!

Pitchbend

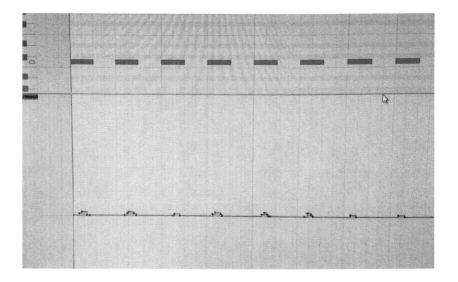

Sometimes adding a tiny bit of pitchbend on each or some notes of your Drop/Groove can make your sound from dull to interesting!
With a 'tiny bit' I mean >> see picture. And this is on a 12 note scale. But try to experiment with this.

TIP 26

EQ

A tip on Equalizing.

Creating depth in your track: (very important!!)

While mixing you also need to concern yourself with the depth of your mix rather then only worry about the stereo imaging.

(Like mixing in 3D)

If you roll off/ cut some of the high frequencies of a sound it will appear further away in your mix.
This used in a proper way you can bring out another element in the same frequency span by boosting those high frequencies.

Like for instance Kick vs Bass.
Or Vocals vs Backing Vocals or mixing guitar parts. Etc...
This way you can emphasize what you want to have in the foreground of your mix or in that particular part of the spectrum.

TIP 27

Compression:

So a lot of people keep asking me about Compressing. How to and what not to!?
First of some basics in a nutshell.
With Compression you can bring down your peak levels and bring up your low levels.
So you reduce the dynamic range so it sounds a bit more fatter.
It's like playing a sound in your house while lowering the ceiling and bringing up the floor.

The basic features on a compressor are:

- Attack: How fast you want the compressor to start compressing

- Release: How long the signal needs to be compressed

- Ratio: How skew your ceiling is. With a ratio of 10:1 meaning a flat roof

- Threshold: How low you want the ceiling to be. So every sound that peaks above your threshold will get compressed

- Make-up Gain: If you use a compressor your volume signals will go down.

With the make up gain you can bring the level up to what it was before compressing. This is the most important thing cause only then you can compare if compression adds anything or not.

So make sure the sound is equally loud when muting or unmuting the compressor.
Beware of the fact that you also boost unwanted signals like low-end noise. So eq this stuff properly.

Each compressor has it's own sound character. You can only learn this by trying them yourselves.

You can find a whole list online with people discussing which one is the best for a typical sound or overall mix.

Compressors (especially analog) create audible sound effects which can sound very pleasing and can do wonders to your overall mix, vocal or sound.

Also cause analog compressors can give you more headroom to start with.

So you can use compression on a sound (drum, bass, synth, guitar, vocal etc.) to make it more present and fatter in your mix.

You can use it to change the envelope of a sound.

You can use it as a limiter

You can use it to create effects. Like compressing sends with reverb or other stuff on it.

You can use it for side-chaining.

You can use it for dynamic EQ'ing

You can use it to give your overall mix a bit more loudness / fatness.

And there are probably other stuff you can do with it, which I don't know of.

I can not give you guys any specific ratio's cause that's different for every sound and every mix you are doing.

However I do advice you to don't overdue it unless you mean to as an effect.

And beware of the fact that your ears get used to the compressed sound very fast.

So keep comparing while mixing otherwise your mix could get more blurry.

TIP 28

Workflow

I always get a lot of questions about workflow.
I can only speak from my point of view about this subject.
And actually I guess it works differently for everybody else.
Anyways,
I don't have a standard way of addressing a new track. They are always different.
Mostly cause of the fact that I have and want to produce in different styles.

Starting a new track:

See what triggers your inspiration. A beat, a melody, a sound, a drop, a vocal.
Take the first thing that inspires you and always work around that and try to make that as finished as possible. Usually the rest will follow automatically.
The track I'm working on now started with the break. I made the layers. Bass, synths and top end. Arranged it properly so that it has a nice start and build up to the drop.
I didn't had any ideas for the drop so I first made some beats which I thought fit the breaks well.
While making the beats you'll form an idea if this is becoming a harder or more progressive type style track. So that narrows the type of drop you are going to make as well.
If you finished the drop then you'll have a whole track in essence.
During the making of the sounds and beats you already start to mix a bit cause that gives you a better idea if it will work or not.

As of now the total idea of the track has to be solid and should already be playable in the clubs more or less.
But,
After this the hard part starts. This is like the last 10% of the track but takes up the most skill and time.

First try to set a logical arrangement for the track.
Then try to fit everything altogether sounding like a complete track.
After that It's all about

- Cutting stuff away (less = More). So don't keep adding things!!!

- Mixing, mixing, mixing

- Make automation for a more natural feel and more control.

- Making effects to mask poor transitions

- Making your track Tight.

- Cut off the tails of effects and sounds which blur to much with other stuff.

- After that Check, Recheck, Check and Recheck again and again.

- Test it in your car , headphone, club, homestereo etc...

TIP 29

Mixing / Mastering

Roll off all the frequencies below +- 100 Hz on all your channels except the kick and the bass.

By doing this you create more breathing space and headroom in your mix! So your mix can become a little bit louder in volume as well.
Besides this you also make sure that you don't boost any unpleasant signals you didn't hear at first during the mastering or gain staging process.

TIP 30

Business

Whenever someone tells you; "This is our standard contract", you know you have options!

TIP 31

Mixing and leveling

Essential part of mixing and leveling;

Take one, or a few tracks that you like, that are in the same sub genre as the one you are producing in.

Use those as a reference point when mixing and gaining your elements. Don't put them over the same master out. Otherwise your 'masterchain' will affect those tracks too.

If you use a lot of multiband or harmonic exitement on tracks it is essential you keep comparing cause you get used to that type of sound very fast. Which makes you think it sounds fat but it could potentially sound like shit when you compare it to those other tracks.

If your track doesn't even come close to the ones you compare it with than try harder and don't send it out untill you have it properly fixed. Always try to make it sound even better then the ones you compare it with!

Mixing / Sounddesign

In today's tip of the week I wanna point out an interesting plugin which not a lot of people know.
The Blue Cat's MB-7 Mixer.

This plugin allows you to split a single signal into 7 frequency bands. Which you can then treat if it were individual tracks. So you can use eq on all frequency channels, play with the stereo field but also you can use up to 4 of your favorite vst's per channel. And use complex side-chaining techniques.
Ideal stuff for making presets for a killer lead sound!
Use it to your advantage.

TIP 33

Reverb:

A few important things about reverb.
You can use reverb to make things sound bigger, more upfront or more in the background.
The most important parameters for your reverb are:

- Pre-Delay:

The time between the original (Dry) sound and the audible reflection and reverb.
So the higher the pre-delay the longer it takes for the reverbsignal to kick in.
If the pre-delay is short it will immediately play a reverbed sound.
So in practice when mixing vocals you want to have a higher pre-delay, so the Dry sound (vocal) will be better understandable.
For big leads I prefer a short pre-delay.

- Reverb Time:

How long would you want the reverb to be.
For creating more presence and putting things upfront in your mix I suggest smaller reverb times.
For creating that big lead you can use a bigger reverb time.

- Size/ Width / and Diffusion of the reverb:

Speak for themselves.

- Reverb Eq:

This one I find important cause you can use this to create a bit more character in your reverb. No high frequencies will cause to make your reverb sound a bit more darker. And putting in more high will make it sound a bit fresher.
I almost never use low frequencies in reverb cause they clutter up your mix. But to much high will also clutter your mix. So don't overdo this

Pro-Tip: Absolute control on your reverb

Use a (side chain) gate on your reverb. That way you have total control of when to open and close the reverbed sound and will make it sound very big and tight. Compress it and Voila!

TIP 34

Automation:

Automation is VERY! Important in your track.

And it's also something what makes the last 10% of your track (to my opinion)

Without it, your track will probably sound dull and lifeless.

I use automation on almost anything.

Here are a few examples.

- Cutting off volumes at the end of build-ups to bring more focus on pre-drop vocals of drum fills.

- Sweeping up your eq or filter to make the sound progressively thinner or darker to create more contrast with the next part of the song.

- Opening up reverbs and delays to create more build up.

- Start an effect and bypass it on certain parts of your track.

- Automation for pitch control

The options are limitless!

Mastering:

Mastering! "The" solution for a proper mix. At least that is what a lot of you think.

Somebody that is sending a demo and saying that the track isn't mastered and that that is the reason why it doesn't sound good is usually ending up in the A&R garbage instantly.

Don't and I mean Don't ever use that as an excuse when sending out a demo.

In dance music mastering is often used as a creative effect to crush the dynamic range and push everything to it's maximum instead of adding a little touch of extra glue or solving some small problems in the final mix. I am also guilty of that cause pushing boundaries is always fun

Anyhow before entering the mastering stage everything should sound good already and properly balanced.

By that I also mean 'ready to test in the club' and to send out as a demo to a record company.

So what do you typically find on a mastering channel for a Dance track.

- Multiband Compressor:

When mixing a track you tend to focuss a bit to much on the mid frequencies. cause that is one of the most difficult areas to mix.

When applying a multi band compressor you can gain control over certain frequency bands and create what some people call a "Smiley" frequency curve. By adding gain reduction in the mid frequencies the track sounds more glued. That makes it more pleasant to listen to.

- Regular Compressor:

Just to create a more overall glued effect.

- Equalizer:

Nowadays with equalizers like for instance Fabfilter 2 you can easily zoom in to little problem areas and fix them.

- Distortion:

Some people use a bit of distortion on there mastering channel to add a bit of warmth.
By using Exciters, Tape saturators, Tubes, Vintage warmers etcetera..

- Limiters:

Keeping your output levels under control.

- A Mono maker / Stereo Widener:

Some plugins have the option to put all the frequencies below a certain point in MONO and with some you can add some stereo width.

For everything goes: Don't overdue it, unless you are using it as a creative effect.
Otherwise if you have to overdue it it's better to adjust your mix.

TIP 36

How to start your mix!

A good way to start your Mix is to trim all your levels down by let's say -10dB.

This gives you instant headroom while mixing your track and provides greater flexibility during your mix down. With more headroom your mix will sound more natural and pleasing

In the end you can always gain it up and bring things to proper levels!

You can use low cpu GAIN vst's to put on all your channels. Works perfectly!

TIP 37

Mono

You know that feeling when your track sounds amazing in your studio and in the club it falls totally apart and out of balance? That could be many things but..
If you are having trouble to mix your stuff in proper balance it definitely helps to mix your volumes and EQ'ing in MONO.
Most (hardware) volume knobs (I use big knob) have a mono button. And every DAW has the same option on the masterbuss.

Press it, mix your volumes right and EQ your stuff like you normally do. Make sure that the frequencies of the different elements don't interfere with each other.
Then when you put the mix back in Stereo you will find that the stereo mix will sound good too. That doesn't work for the other way around.
After that you can adjust some of the placements in the stereo field but also keep checking back in Mono and adjust if necessary.

TIP 38

Writers Block and Creativity

In the studio it's important to keep your creativity flowing.
Here are a few pointers which you can take into consideration.

First off. It's always better to get into the studio when you have an idea.
If you don't know where to begin, I usually grab a piano and start playing a theme.
If the writing of a melody doesn't work for you then go make some beats or focus on the drop part.

Things that also can help boost the inspiration is to listen to some older classics.
I listen a lot to the house music I was growing up with. back in the 90's.
Sometimes I go thru stock presets of a synth to see if there's anything interesting.
You could go online and find the weirdest vst there is and try stuff with that.

You could listen to other songs and try to analyze them. In that way you are learning as well and getting inspired.

One of the most important things I learned is that when you feel creative is to write as many melodies as you can. Not just focus on one track at that moment. Cause then when you are a bit uninspired you can always fall back on something you made earlier. Also when you hear back your older melody you remember what you wanted to do with that in the first place. Same goes for making drops.

Creativity always comes and goes and to my opinion it's the discipline (and talent) you put into it which gives you the studio output you are looking for.

If nothing of this helps it's better to go to the beach and try the next day

Production tip: Making a cool bass

Take a sub bass and play your melody with that one. Cutoff all the high until at least 1.5 kHz.

Compress the sub bas to keep it under control. and cutoff everything beneath 40 Hz.

Make sure it's mono. Put a bit of side-chain on it. So your kick can stand out in comparison to the Sub bassline.

Now Copy that melody to another synth on which you make an 2 voice oscillator saw wave.

Cutoff a bit of the low end. Let's say everything under 100 hZ. Put a stereo expander on it and then distort it big time (but keep it pretty natural sounding).

Blend the two together and you will have a bassline that cuts thru everything.

TIP 40

How to get your record signed!

I get this question a lot. I am not really sure how to answer this one.
However keep the following in mind.
Since it became affordable and possible to make dance music from your attic, everybody loves to give it a shot in becoming famous and be the next gen producer and or DJ.
As a result record companies are overthrown with demo's.
And with their experience they can probably tell within seconds if the track has potential or that its crap.
Believe me when I say that they get a lot of bad music.
I think we can safely say there is a ratio of 1 to a 100 tracks that sound ok.
Out of a 1000 tracks they find ten good ones which might get signed.
So for starters the competition is fierce.

Here are a few absolute DONT'S:

- Don't send partial demo's

- Don't send unfinished demo's

- NEVER I repeat NEVER!!!!! say that your demo is not mixed or mastered yet.

- Don't write full length letters with your whole life story.

If A&R's never reply to your email and If DJ's never respond to your demo's that's, and I'm sorry to say it, cause they don't like it.

Here's a few DO's:

- Send finished demo's. Or at least present them as finished.

- Introduce yourself shortly. Name, maybe a small discography, email address and telephone number and maybe a small support list from big DJ's.

- If you want to stand out from all those other people make sure your demo sounds perfect and even better then your favorite tracks.

- Try to make it original sounding.

- Create a good online profile for yourself. Get a few head shots and create some good looking social media pages.

If you have made a good track in which A&R's believe they will sign your track!!! They will probably even embrace you and try to hear more stuff and sign you exclusive
Quality will "Always float to the top".

Even if A&R's pass on your track but it's still a killer track, there will always be a DJ which hears your demo on for instance Soundcloud and gets in contact with you.

Here's a tip for what I sometimes do.
I put a small 'tease' MP3 of the demo with only the break and the drop. And add the download link to the full version in the email.

TIP 41

LOUDNESS

is all about perception.

It's a subject that is pretty complicated and on which we can write books about.

But that's just boring so I will try and keep this as short and essential for you as possible.

When you make a track, your own taste will determine how your song will sound.

Do you want a compressed type of sound or do like a more open sound?

Do you want to keep a bigger loudness range in your track or do you want to sound equally hard during the whole track.

If you strive for certain loudness from a reference track it can help to do the following things.

Play the track with for instance the meter bridge from ozone 5 on it. This will show you the loudness range of your favorite track.

It shows it in 3 steps. Peak, short-term & integrated. Then you can compare those numbers with the ones from your track.

Now how to get that same loudness as your reference track?

There is a handy tool for that. Called the 'perception controller' from for instance "meter plugs".

This plugin let's you set the 'LUFS' (loudness units full scale) the same for all your tracks.

The great thing about that is that you can truly hear how a track is mixed! Which makes it easier for you to adjust your own mix to your reference mix.

So with the perception controller you will have an audible guide and with the ozone 5 meter you will have a visual guide.

TIP 42

Know when to stop!

Know when to stop and to get out of the studio!

It's important to know when 'enough is enough' studiotime.
For instance, now it's Christmas! So get out of your studio and spend some time with family and friends .

Merry Christmas!

TIP 43

Widening up your sound

On great request....

10 Ways to widen up your sound:

Some of them were already discussed but it's still a nice overview.

- 1: Stereo Delay: Use a stereo delay with a very short delay time. between 2-10 ms.

- 2. Split Equalizing: Use an equalizer in which you can equalize the left and right channel separately. This will slightly widen up your sound.

- 3. Stereo Enhancers: There are a lot of stereo enhancement plugins. I personally play around a lot with the ones from Waves, Brainworx and Izotope.

- 4. M/S Equalizing. see tip #19 for explanation.

- 5. Split your stereo channel into two separate channels and pan hard left & right.

- 6. Put two delays on your channel, pan one hard left and the other hard right.

- 7. Put two reverbs in two different aux busses. Pan one hard left the other hard right. Cut off all the lows from the reverb. Experiment with the reverb settings. From there on you can also put a compressor behind the reverb or a side chain effect to give it a bit more edge. Some say this works great with smaller convolution reverbs.

- 8. Formant Shifting: Split the signal into two separate tracks. Then apply formant shifting (Shifting of a frequency range) in an opposite direction to either one or both tracks. You can do this for instance in Melodyne.

- 9. Put some distortion in a send buss with some stereo enhancers on top and mix that in with the original sound.

- 10. Be sure that you check your mono compatibility regularly since these effects will most likely mess with that when you apply to much.

That's why it can be very helpful to do a lot of these stereo enhancements via busses (Auxes). So you will be sure that your mix will hold in Mono.

TIP 44

Ambient noises or background action in a track

When creating an intro/ outro of a track it sometimes help to make use of ambient sounds for a couple of reasons
to fill up the frequency spectrum, to give the track some character and build up excitement, or to create a minimum sound reference level.
To do this you can use anything actually. Common things like white noise, stabs with lots of reverb on it, sample pack fx's or your actual theme sound but then put in a filter with some cool effects on it etc.

Endless opportunities. You can use all your effects and creativity for this kind of stuff.
My personal preference always goes to "airy" type sounds cause those tend to open up your mix in a good way.
Airy type sounds are sounds like: Choirs, nature sounds, campfire sounds etc..
I even once used a sample of a bunch of crickets in the forrest with some endless reverb and side chaining to get the job done
Always mix in these sounds at a soft volume. You barely need to hear them in your mix but if you take them away you are missing something...

Physics / EQ / Acoustics

Each note on your keyboard corresponds with a frequency and therefore a wavelength.
For instance the key C3 corresponds with the frequency 130,81.

You can use this to your advantage when mixing certain sounds.
As many of you have learned EQ sweeping to find the right frequencies to cut or to add you can also use this scheme as a reference point.

Let's say you are working with a guitar sound in the key of A and you want to give it more natural warmth and body you can for instance boost a bit at 110 & 220 & 440 Hertz with a higher Q.
Or if you want to give it a bit more presence you can add a bit of 7kHz.
This can also help you to prioritize sounds which are in the same frequency range in a mix. To bring them more forward or backward into your mix.
Also
When knowing all these key vs frequencies you can find out which frequency in your studio is causing problems while mixing. For instance in the Fabfilter Pro Q2 Equalizer you can select the key.

TIP 46

Subtractive and additive EQ'ing in commercial dance music.

I don't want to start the discussion on which is better. Just want to give you my personal opinion on this matter.

In the creative phase of making sounds I use everything necessary to achieve the sound I want for in a drop, break, whatever.
So I usually end up Boosting a lot of frequencies with equalizers distortion etcetera. Once I have my sounds made I usually bounce them and start the mix down process fresh or put them into a group bus.

Normally in the mix down process I use a lot of Subtractive EQ'ing. The advantages of Subtractive EQ'ing are numerous.

- You create more headroom
- Mix will sound more natural
- You keep your master buss under control
- It's easier to lift out a particular synth when cutting out the others.
- When mixing vocals into your track it's better and easier to cut a bit of the instrument frequencies which clash with the vocal. Instead of boosting the vocal to make it sound more unnatural.

Of course I also boost frequencies in the mix down. But more to create air or a more warm feel in the mix.

I know plenty of producers who do otherwise, but this is just how I do it.

The moment you know in which frequency span a certain instrument/ synth has it's sweetspot you also know which frequencies you can cut. Always cut away frequencies by listening to the whole mix. Not just solo'd. A lot of instruments have the tendency that when you cut away some frequencies in the low/low-mid it naturally boosts in the mid-high/high.

TIP 47

Working with a musical (business) partner

Everything seems easier when you do it with more people.
Making tracks becomes easier when you have a sparring partner.
Even DJ'ing can be easier when you always travel together and you can share thoughts and experiences.
Especially at the start of your career you don't think about any future consequences.

- Are you both equally ambitious?

- Are you both equally talented?

- Do you complement each other?

- Can you both execute as much as needed?

Is one person always thinking about getting home while the other one wants to travel more?
If you don't make business agreements at the start of your career, chances are that when money and fame comes in, the relationship between you becomes skew and things can go wrong.
So if you start out with two or more be sure to discuss your future 'dream' plans and be sure to put them on paper concurrently with the obligations and splits you both promise.
Don't forget that the "Music Industry" is a business and your business partner shouldn't be your best friend. People need time apart and there own friends.
It's a hard lesson, but a valuable one.

TIP 48

Income streams for DJ's and Producers

As a starting Producer/ DJ it's important to know in which ways you can make some money in this industry. The better you know this, the sooner you can start to make your hobby into your profession.

All these terms are based on Dutch/ European law.
In the states or elsewhere they sometimes use different terms. But you'll get the point.

1. Sale Royalties:

Getting a percentage on the sales of your music.
Usually split into
Real product: Vinyl, cd's, albums and
Digital: Downloads, Streams, Youtube plays etc.
Sub/ Thirdparty licensing: Meaning, when a different country or record company license the right from the record company or directly from the artist to release and exploit the music.

2. Copyright

Copyright is there to prevent that somebody uses a piece of work created by someone else without their permission.
The rights to make your work public are also called exploitation rights. Most music authors choose to assign these to a publisher. Sometimes in return for an advance. Depending on how big of an artist you are.
Copyrights are paid for when your music is being played on the radio. When your music is being used in movies and series and games. When your music is performed during big events etceteras.
Since the digital era these incomes are getting even bigger then sale royalties.
Terms often used here are sync rights, sync licenses, performing rights, composer/lyricist and publisher.

3. Neighbouring rights / Performer's right only applies to European law or those who apply the convention of Rome.

Let's say you were hired to play the keyboard during a recording session. The song becomes a hit. But you didn't produce the track and you didn't write it.
You can still see some money in the form of neighboring rights.
In that case you will receive revenue when played on the radio/tv or when being performed on stage.

4. Bookings fees

This is probably the biggest revenue to earn these days. Receive money to perform as a DJ or as a performing Artist.

5. Flat fees

These are fees that a music or vocal producer could get paid for producing music.
Let's say you want Dr. Luke to produce your next pop single he's going to charge you.

6. Sponsor and Merchandise deals

In the United States already a big business for years. In the EU it's still upcoming.
Connect your profile to a brand and receive revenue for that.
Examples these days are clothing, headphones, software plugins etc.

But all this is actually nothing compared to the thing that got started in 2008.
In 2008 record companies were looking into the future predicting that sales would fall thanks to the up come of digital and illegal downloading. Streaming service Spotify made his attendance. But for Spotify to succeed it needed content of course. So Spotify got his content from SONY BMG / Warner Music / Universal Music and EMI among others.
Now let's fast forward to 2017.
Spotify has plans to go public and is valued at a price of currently 8 Billion Dollars.
The thing that got my attention is that those content suppliers I was talking about all got a stake in the company.

These percentages are rumors but still likely to be true according to the financial times.
Sony BMG 5,8%
Universal Music 4,8%
Warner Music 3,8%
EMI 1,9%

Now how much of this money do you think is falling back to the artists they have signed?
I'll let you do the math and figure out who's the real MVP in the Music Industry!

Monitor volumes

This is a very important tip which sets the base for everything!
If you want to mix your leads or whatever in a Fat way. You first need to know what Fat is, and sounds in your studio/room.
When you are mixing your track you need to find a monitor volume for you that works.

The best is to put your volumes not to hard to prevent ear fatigue or even damage.
When experiencing ear fatigue your perception of sound will change. So beware of that.
When mixing down a clubtrack it's often tempting to put the volume up of your speakers to get that real clubfeel.

The best thing you can do is to mix every track in your studio at a constant volume.
It will help you to know and better learn the loudness of your own and other tracks.

I've marked a certain point on my bigknob controller.
This way you can get used to the sound pressure levels.
In general you could say that the bigger the speakers the more sound pressure you have, the lower you can keep the volume .
The more tracks you will mix this way the better they will sound.
Cause you will learn very fast how a mix should sound at that volume.
This way you can also rely on your ears during the mix down instead of metering.

I put the volumes way up to listen if the drop makes the impact I am aiming for.
Or just to mix the kick drum.

Also near the end of the mix down I put the volume super low to hear if I can filter out and hear all the different elements in the track like the kick, bas, clap, HI hats, leads, strings, vox etc..

If you can hear them all in a clean way then you have made a proper mix balance between all elements. Of course be sure to reference with different monitors or headphones

Phase Part 1

Phase

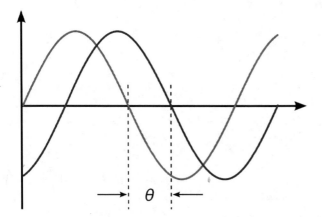

First some theory:

Phase is a term for where a waveform is in it's cycle.

If you put 2 sine waves on top of each other you going to double the amplitude.

However if you shift 1 of those 2 sine waves they will get out of phase. And if you put it 180 degrees out of phase, the waveforms will cancel each other out.

Phase will sound like a hollow or comb-filtered sound.

See photo.

Phase problems usually exist when recording (drums) with multiple microphones.

In dance music it's more likely to happen when you stack multiple low sounds, like basses on top of each other.

The best ways to avoid this if you want to use multiple layers is to mix in frequency ranges.

Sub - Low - Mid - High. This way you prevent clashing.

Best way still is to use only one sound for the lower bass and one for the high bas to cut through a mix.

And then you can use parallel compression for instance (tip #22) to fatten things up without any phase problems.

Of course there are also 'Phase Alignment' Tools vst's available who can do the trick for you. Google and find!

Also if you would use the meter bridge in Ozone for instance and you open up the Phase scope/ Phase Meter you can also visually see if there are any problems. If the scope is to scattered on material that should be more in mono then you can see that.

If you look at a phase meter you need to know that

0 value is perfect stereo

+1 value is perfect mono

-1 value is perfect out of phase.

It's best to score in the upper 1's.

Phase Part 2

Mono compatibility:

Stereo means that there are time arrival differences between the Left and the Right channel.
This way it creates a sense of dimension for the human ear which enhances your listening experience bla bla bla...

So here's a stereo image of a left and right channel that are in phase.

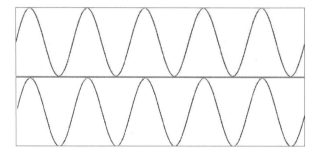

And here's one that's out of phase

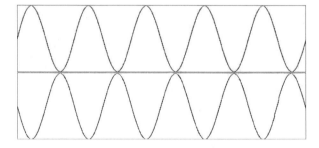

Now the one that's out of phase will only become noticeable when you press your mono button.
Then it will either disappear or looses a lot of power and will sound hollow.

That's why it is so important to constantly check your mixes for mono compatibility.

Why would we even wanna have mono compatibility?

The sound systems in clubs still have a mono setup.

Because of the fact that the music needs to sound equal in all areas of the club.

If it would be in stereo then you would only perceive it when you are standing in just the right place.

Also some radio stations that in are in an area of lower reception will switch to Mono to give a better signal.

And if you want to play your new track for your grandmother on her old radio it's probably also a mono device.

Then why we just don't mix everything in Mono?

Cause you also want to listen to music in your car, on your stereo on your computer etc..

And these are all stereo.

Troubleshooting:

If your mix sounds really bad in mono you can try to use Mid/Side Eq on your problem channels or master out and use the 'Mid' function to see if you can improve the mono mix. This will usually do the trick

Where do I place my subwoofer?

An interesting way of finding the right place for your subwoofer in your home studio is the following.

First make sure you set the crossover around 85Hz. This makes sure that it will not interfere with any mid-range content and it stays unlocatable. Then turn your sub to average levels.

Now place the subwoofer on the ground on your listening position. So pull away your studio chair and replace it with the sub.
Play out your reference tracks of which you know have a well mixed bass. Use a couple of reference tracks in different keys.
Then go on your hands and knees and start crawling around and behind your mixing desk. Eventually you will find a place where the bass response sounds the best.
That will be the spot where you place your subwoofer.

TIP 53

Layering Synths Part 2

You can read Tip 16 for part 1

Creating the stereo image for a layered synth.
Try to create some sort of 'hand fan' of sound.
So the lower sounds in the middle.
The main synth a bit wider or even fully panned L and R.
And the character sound really wide with some effects.
In that case it would be like a wall of sound coming your way.
When you mix these three layers, always solo them as a group and compress them as a group as well for better results.
If the sounds are well made and chosen they should blend easy together with just some volume, eq and a group compress.

Loudness

Sure let's talk some more about loudness since recent events.

First off, in dance music there is a difference between using loudness plugins to maximize your mix or using loudness plugins to create a certain sound which some artist can claim as a signature sound.

The trick is to get a loud mix without creating to much distortion or any harsh sounds and keeping it dynamic.

Sometimes when I listen to Sirius XM for instance and you hear those loud mastered tracks 'Digital full Scale' mixed after each other over the radio compressor. It starts to sound really boring and monotonous cause the difference between the loudness in the breaks and drops are gone and you hear so much more audible effects due to the radio compressor and the lack of good mixing.

So the greater the difference between loud and quiet the greater the impression of the loudness is.

So again some tips for creating louder tracks.

If the drop sounds really loud that doesn't necessarily have to be a bad thing.

But a good tip would be to create a volume drop in the build up. So the impact of the drop will be bigger.

Also it's nice to create a bit more volume differences in the break compared to the drop.

Just put the volume down a bit.

Don't over-use the multiband compressor/ Soundgooddizer. This will make your sound louder, but also more harsh.

Also make sure to cut all frequencies, which aren't necessary for that instrument/sound.

This will create so much more headroom, which will give you a louder perception.

Also mixing wider can create the illusion of louder mix. So panning and stereo enhancing without affecting the mono field is important as well.

And one of the most important things is actually to choose a good sound from the start, which is already loud and full so you don't have to enhance it all that much.

So yes a loud track will make a bigger impact in the club but even more when it also has a dynamic range.

TIP 55

How to save CPU

Nothing more annoying when working on a project and your computer starts hitching. When you zoom in & out your screen slows down and your sound card starts hanging. So here's a few tips to keep your DAW fast at all times.

- Work with effects on your send busses instead of your insert busses. This way you only have to use two reverbs and 2 delays for the whole project.

- Freeze your instrument: This is a function most vst synths have. This way you can not alter the sound anymore but it saves a lot of cpu.

- Bounce your sound into an audio track. If you made a cool sound in a vst synth. Bounce it to audio and delete the synth.

- Work with group editing. Route your sounds to a bus and process from there instead of dealing with all channels separately.

- Make an archive of your audio samples. (see tip 12)

- Increase your buffer size. If your buffer size is low your cpu will start spiking soon. But in the beginning of the project you will have no latency. By increasing the buffer size to 256 or 512mb you will have some latency but you can work on bigger projects.

- If you use native instrument sound banks or banks from East-West or something similar it can help to put your sound banks on a SSD disk and load from there.

- Use only low cpu plugins. You can find reviews on everything and there are always plugins who can do an evenly well job but by using less CPU.

Harmonic Exciter

Harmonic exciters can add subtle harmonic distortion in your high frequency signals.

This effect can significantly brighten up your mix if well used.

You can also use this effect on the lower frequencies to make sure your bass will sound as a bass on smaller speakers as well.

There are a lot of good harmonic exciters but my favorites are the ones from Aphex & Ozone.

Vocoder

A vocoder analyzes your voice spectrum and applies it to a second signal. Usually a synthesizer.

It's mainly used to create cool vocal effects like in "Daft Punks – Harder Better Faster Stronger".

It's also a great tool to use for background vocal effects.

The funny thing is that you can sing very monotone while playing the keys to make it very musical. Perfect for those who can't sing but still want to get cool results.

I've used it a couple of times to create pre-drop vocals. You could use it also as a similar tool to create the chopped vocal sound.

You would record a monotone long sound of yourself...Like aahhhhhh-hhh and then you can play your own midi pattern with your own melody and get creative.

I use "The Mouth" by native instruments for this.

Transient Designers

This is a plugin that is easily forgotten by most producers but comes in very handy in a lot of occasions. With a transient designer you can shape the transients of a sound. Usually the Attack and the Sustain.

Let's say your kick is not punching thru your mix the right way. If you boost the attack on the transient designer you will immediately hear a difference.

you can also use it the other way around. Let's say there is a hard spike in the attack of a sound you just sampled. You can easily make that disappear by turning down the Attack on the transient designer.

It also comes in handy when you want to cut away some room verb. In that case you can shorten the sustain of the sound so it sounds a lot tighter. I often use it when layering synths and when I want to make sure they all have kind of the same Attack and Sustain. So it sounds more like one sound.

Yes, this all can also be achieved by using compressors and gates. But this is much easier.

TIP 59

Dynamic EQ-ing

Dynamic EQ-ing is a handy tool for fixing certain frequency problems. It's a very precise tool which can be hard to master and certainly isn't used in most occasions. You can control the Gain of an EQ band instead of a frequency range like in a multi band compressor.
It is mostly used when De-essing vocals.
So when there is too much sibilance, the high frequencies are compressed and this way turned down a bit.
if you cut a frequency in a dynamic EQ, it won't apply that cut until the frequency crosses a threshold.
So use it to flatten out any annoying frequency, which occurs non-randomly.
Like vocals, drumloops, samples.
You can also use it to spice up a kick.
For instance when the kick punches over a certain threshold it automatically gaines a bit in the high-mid but only at the point of the kicks attack.
So it then won't clash with your other elements.

You can also use it to create a sort of dynamic side chaining effect on your kick bass. Which makes them blend even better.

TIP 60

Export reference

For this weeks tip I have a very simple but super important one. You can mix in the highest resolution possible for best results but the consumer will most likely play your track in an 'MP3 320 Kbps' format. So make sure you also make a 320kbps Bounce and test that one on all your speakers, headphones, earplugs, car stereo etc.. If that one sounds good you are done.

TIP 61

Problems in the high end

Sometimes when you are using to much high Eq or an exciter to spark things up it could sound nasty.

An alternative way to fix this problem is to put a Soundreducer / Bitcrusher on the sound / instrument which is causing the 'nasty high' sound. This will reduces the harshness of the high but without affecting the finished feel of the overall mix.

TIP 62

Mastering

So a cool tip on mastering.

In tip 45 we discussed the EQ-ing i.c.w. the key of a track vs the frequency chart.

You can apply this to your mastering as well.

Say you have made a track in G, but the overall sound isn't totally in the right spectrum you wish it would be in. you can mold it a bit by using that frequency chart and cutting and / or boosting the specific frequencies which are in the key of G.

Play with it and see what it does with your final master!

How to make a scary soundeffect or interesting buildup

How to make a scary sound effect. Something which you could definitely hear in a horror score. Now effects can be made in a million ways. So this is just one example and I will only cover the basics from this one. After that you can start adding whatever you like to it.

So first of i would like to start with a Nexus Piano. (I've used the XP Dance Orchestra> PN Piano Soft). You can use whatever sound for this of course. Now play a few scary notes and put them in your daw. Put the release to almost max, and put on some arena Reverb. Now to make the piano sound really scary you can use Tip 79 (detuning an oscillator sound in cents) and exaggerate it. This will create the famous horror piano.

So that's it for the sound.
Now let's put a reverb on an insert channel and look for the "Hold" or "Infinite Sustain" switch. This switch will hold your reverb sound until infinity. Now automate that so it will activate on the last note of your scary melody. After this we put in a pitchshifter. (I've used the one from Waves). Now slowly pitch up the reverb signal for as long as you like. Maybe 4 bars or so? Now you already get that build up/ scary sustain kinda vibe. To make it a bit more grittier we gonna add the H-Delay from waves on the insert as well. Put the delay on MS and set a high feedback (over 100). Now automate the dry/wet signal of the delay in a similar curve as you did with the pitchbend. So now when the sound reaches a higher pitch it gets grittier. Which creates more suspense as well.

Of course when it's not halloween you can use these type of effects as buildups in your productions.

TIP 64

Templates

Starting your track with a template could give you a great headstart to immediately being creative instead of setting things up first. Which can take up precious time.

Try to keep improving your templates so you don't get stuck in a fixed pattern.

A template could consist of a few audiotracks with inserts on them like gain control, EQ, Compressors. And a few tracks with some of your favorite synthesizers and drum computers / Samplers.

Most DAW's are drag & drop these days. So you could also save your insert settings and name them for their specific function. That way you can easily drag in a mix setting on the fly and start tweaking from a great starting point.

Song Tempo

Sometimes it's fun to play around with the tempo of a track to see what it does to the overall feel. When doing this you sometimes create whole new genres like ,
Lento Violento, Speedy Bubbling: or maybe the best example of them all : the slowing down of Afrojacks remix of DJ Chuckie's - moombah. Which also set a base for the moombahton genre.

My point to this is to always target your track to the audience you want to reach but also play (test) it out a different tempo. It just might even sound better.
I think the most recent example of this is Kygo which produces tracks in around 100 bpm to 114 bpm.

TIP 66

Speed

Sometimes it's important to create the feel of speed in a track.
A good tip to help create that is as follows:

If you have a Kick in your mix already. Place a "tok" on a different track on top of the kick. A "tok" would be like a kick or a tom or a short hihat. But then extremely shortened, so that you only hear the attack.
Remember I told you about the formula to calculate delay and decay times? 60000 divided by the BPM of the track.

In case of a 128 bpm track that would be 468,75 ms for a quarter delay. Now divide that again thru 4 to get the 16th delay. (=117,18 ms).
Now put a delay of 117 ms on the "Tok" and listen what happens to your mix.

Play around to see what other results you can get.

TIP 67

Mixing

A great trick to give your drop some more impact is by using the Mid-Side EQ.
Group your drop synths to one channel and use the mid-side eq on that channel to cut of the low with the MID Eq.

The advantage with this trick is that you create more space for the kick and bass to punch thru without making your leads sound to thin.

TIP 68

Mixing Kick & Bass vs Drop Melody

This mixing tip comes particularly in handy while mixing a progressive style drop.

And it's an alternative or an addition to the previous mixing tip (nr.67) Normally you would put a side chain on the melody to give it more energy and to let it sit better in the mix.

But if you then still having some trouble to get the kick & bass punch thru you could add a Multiband Sidechain on the lead sound.
In which you only side chain the lower end of the spectrum. Let's say a split frequency between 500 & 1000 Hz.

This creates even more space for the low-end (Kick & Bass) and makes your mix sound better.

Folder Tracks

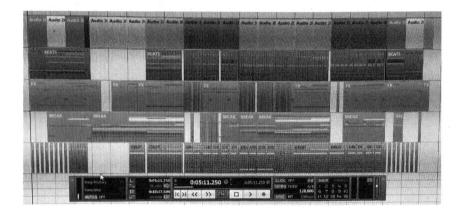

After finishing your track it is important to clean up your track. Delete everything you didn't use. Put all your files in a separate 'backup' folder. It could take a while before signing and releasing that track. And sometimes weeks after you finished the track you are also asked to make some final adjustments. If you open your old projects and it's a complete mess it could take you forever to make adjustments since you are already busy creating your next hit. But when you open up an old track and you left it totally organized you can start right away.

If you teach yourself a standard way of cleaning up your track your workflow will improve drastically.

If you look at my picture. I always use color coding for the arrangement. For me it's easy to see in an instant where the drop or the beginning of a segment is. After that I put my tracks together in folders. In this case: Beats/ FX/ Break/ Drop When you open up the 'Beats' folder you will see all your beat stems. (loops, claps, hihats, kick, toms etc..) It's also easy then to Solo or mute a complete folder. This gives you a fast flexibility while mixing certain parts of your track. Meaning you can focus on all the 'Drop' stems in one instance.

TIP 70

The Noise Gate

A noise gate attenuates a signal below a set threshold.
It's an insert effect you probably don't use that much.
Normally used to filter out the spill sound from a Drum set recording for example.

However it's a nice effect to use in Dance music as well.
In one of my first tips I told you that you can control the tail of your sound with it. Especially when you use a lot of reverb that can come in handy to keep everything tight. Meaning, you can create a Big sound without drowning your mix in a continuous reverb.
But you can also use it to clean up your sampled material. To mask noise and crackle you sometimes get when compressing old samples.
And lately I'm also using it on arpeggios. To make them sound even tighter. Which in the end gives you a clearer mix.

Play around with it and see what it can add to your mix.

TIP 71

Midrange

The 250 Hz till 4kHz area also known as the midrange is very important for your mixing. If mixed right you create the most energy in your track possible which translates well to every system.

A few tips to prevent muddy midrange mixes.

- Cut all the high of the low. Your bass operates somewhere in the area of 40 to 400 Hz. Meaning you can cut everything above 400 Hz without affecting the overall feel of the bass. But this way you create more space for the Mid frequencies.

- Use a good reference system. You ever wondered why every High-end studio has those old Yamaha NS-10 Speakers? Not cause they sound amazing. But cause they exaggerate the mid spectrum. Making it easier to mix the Mids. If it sounds great on Yamaha NS-10's it sounds great everywhere.I don't have NS-10's. I use the Sennheiser HD 650 (or 800) for this. They pretty much do the same although you cannot define the stereo field that well on headphones.

- And last, put your volume way down in a way that you can barely hear your mix. And then try to listen if you can distinguish every sound in your mix. Or in this case the mid spectrum.

TIP 72

Wide Stereo Lead

A nice way to widen up your lead sound is to open up two synths with the same preset. Pan one hard left and the other one hard right. And then create a small difference to one (synth) side by adding some chorus or for instance an LFO.

TIP 73

Layering

how to keep your mix feeling more lively and adding more body to a sound. A good tip for this is to double your synth with a live instrument. For example: Complement your synthesizer string with for instance a long horn sound. This will add much more live feel to the track. And makes it stand out even more.

Muddiness

Here's a little assignment for you today. Take your latest mix you have been working on. Put an Eq on the master buss. Set a Bell EQ with a semi-narrow Q and boost it a lot. Sweep it between 250Hz & 500Hz until it sounds really bad. Then flip the EQ and cut that portion with a dB or 3.

Is your overall mix sounding better now?

How to give your Lead sound a little extra spice

Try to put a short hihat on every note of your main melody. This short tick sound will let your melody pop out even more. Instead of a short hihat you can also use white noise. This creates also some extra harmonics on top of your lead.

Mix them in very gently. Just hard enough that you miss them when muted.

Career

During your career as a DJ/Producer it is very important to surround yourself with people who you can really trust and from who you know they serve your best interest. Your 'team' is the addition to your career. Don't be fooled by all the people who suck up to you or promise you everything, despite it being very tempting.

Be sure to put promises in writing so you can fall back if things go bad.

In the end this is a music industry which evolves around one thing, which is money. And money (and fame) causes a lot of trust and backstabbing issues.

So enjoy what you do and treat your trustworthy team as family with mutual respect. That is THE way to become succesfull in every aspect of the word and have a lot of fun as well. Which is also equally important.

But!!! Don't forget it is YOU in the first place that has to deliver a good show and good music. Your 'team' can not do that for you.

••

However if all might fail we can always do like the famous French general Napoleon once said: 'If you wish to be a success in the world, promise everything, deliver nothing'

Vocal Side-Chain

So today I needed to mix in a vocal on top of an instrumental. The vocal seemed to disappear a bit in the mix. So I took a compressor and put it on the Instrumental. (Track 1) Then I made a ghosttrack (track 2) ,output routed to sidechain, and placed the vocal on that track. I've put the side-chain on of the compressor and set a small threshold, midsize attack and longer release. And I've placed the vocal track (track 3) in the mix also. Now everytime the vocal is playing the instrumental gets a little ducked which makes the vocal stand out more.

Problem solved.

Rhytmic Gating

You probably all know how to create that famous stutter effect. But you almost always use that as a 1/8th note or 1/16th note effect. But have you ever tried "Rhytmic Gating"?

Let's say you a have a string on track 1. And a drumloop on track 2. If you put a Noise-Gate with the sidechain on, on track 1 and route the input of the sidechain to the drumloop You would then make a rhytmic string that follows the transients of the drumloop. You can play around with the threshold/ attack/ release of the gate to make it fit to your liking.

You can use any rhytmic groove/ sound you want. So be creative with this. You can get some cool results.

A 'Lively' sound

That is quit a vague term. But still important to my opinion. I think its meaning is adding a certain richness to a sound. Or to make your mix sound less static.

A good way of doing this is by detuning the Cents (1/100 of a Semi-tone) of the layers of a sound.

An easy example would be for instance; Take a sound from the Nexus Vst. (press 'Mix' and the tab 'Lay")

Now sometimes you will see that sounds are build from seperate layers which you can also detune. If you detune the sounds a couple of Cents each, you will notice a difference in the liveliness of the sound.

Play around with it and see what it does to your sound.

For the experts out here. This effect is kinda similar to a chorus effect but it ain't a chorus. I think the technical term would be "off-key" or "Floating".

TIP 80

EQ'ing before or after Compression

So a lot of things have been written on this subject. And It's definitely a matter of taste In general you could say that an EQ before Compression would give you the chance to get away of all the mud so that the compressor only triggers on what you feed into it. That gives a more natural processed sound.

Also if you want to exaggerate stuff in your mix it's also better to do that before the compressor so that it still cuts through your mix without sounding to harsh.

However if you want your EQ not to interact with your compressor then you should place it after.

And you could always place one before and one after the compressor.

Superwide

A wider mix can be important to create space for all the elements that make up your mix. With some key ingredients in the middle, like the Kick, Bass & Vocal. And some ingredients that should be wider to not interfere with those key elements in the middle.

So back at Tip 43 we talked about how to make your mix sound wider.

But here's another great tip which you should definitely try.

It's kinda similar to Tip 72 but with a Twist.

Take for instance the lead sound that you are using. Copy the vst so you have two identical synths. Now make both sounds Mono. You can use the BX_Control V2 or S1 imager for instance to make this happen. Now pan one channel hard left and one channel hard right. Now you have a real stereo feel, which will also sound amazing on your headphones Now you can mix it as you like.

Now to make it sound even wider and better you can adjust the delay of the channel. I think every DAW has this function where you can adjust the timing of the channel a bit. (So it starts later or sooner in comparison to the other channels). See photo.

Now put the left channel on -8 miliseconds and the right channel to +8 miliseconds. This is enough to make it sound wider without causing any problems in your mix.

Try it and compare it with the original lead you had.

TIP 82

Creating your own sound

Every artist wants to distinct themselves from others.

A good way of doing that is to create your own customized presets for your mix busses. A lot of people always scroll thru there eq, reverb, compressor or whatever mixplugin standardpresets to find there best setting. But if you put a good amount of time in it to create your own you are also creating a signature sound for yourself. Which eventually will be the best starting point for all your mixes.

TIP 83

How to Arrange your track?

So you have made a great melody and a good idea for a drop. But how do you put all those together and make a full track out of it?

Here are some tips you can apply to make things a bit easier.

First and most important. Find a track from which you like the arrangement and you know that that will work in a club or festival.

Try to analyze that arrangement and try to understand why that works. Maybe even create a current top 5 of tracks that work and have a cool arrangement and see what fits your idea.

You can then place the track in your DAW and use colorcoding for the BARS to set out an arrangement which you could follow along.

You can use terms like INTRO / BREAK / BUILDUP / DROP / BRIDGE to make an easy guidance for yourself. See example.

Make sure every part of a track sounds equally interesting. And keep clear distinctions between the different parts. But still keep it cohesive. How to keep it cohesive? That's where the creativity comes in. Fills, Effects, Hints, Intertwining Melodies etc..

If the transitions between parts are to abrupt. Then it has to be for a reason. Otherwise try to make it more smooth.

In the end the track should flow natural.

TIP 84

Speaker placement

A helpfull first guideline of speakerplacement. Now every room is different so you always need to experiment. But here are three simple guidelines to start with!

- Speakers need to be as far apart from each other as you are from them.

- Speakers need to be at least 60 cm away from your backwall.

- Make sure that the distance between the side and the backwall are unequal.

This way you ensure the most accurate response. After this you can decide in what way you can improve the acoustics of the room.

Or when you have acoustic measurements of your room to begin with you can also calculate where the best place is to put your speakers based on the first reflections of the problem frequencies in your room.

TIP 85

Panning

Which type of panning is better.

Symmetrical or Asymmetrical?

I think the key thing here is that your mix sounds well balanced. I personally only use Asymmetrical panning on character type sounds in breaks. If I put a reverby type piano and pan that one 80% to the left then I still want to have something compensating on the right side. Preferably something in the same frequency range. Maybe a violin type sound or so. Make sure your amplitude of both sounds are around the same. If you do that right you create a more wide spacious atmosphere for in the break.

For the drop I would not recommend it. Just try and keep things Symmetrical for max impact on the dance floor.

BUT! If you make music pure for listening purposes you can absolutely be more creative in this. (like for instance U2 – Vertigo).

For the rest if you are (symmetrical) panning your mix be aware that you not only pan straight in the middle and hard left and hard right. Cause that way you can create holes in mixing image.

Use everything in your mixing image to create that wall of sound:

- UpFront and in the Middle

- Hard Left , Hard Right

- Behind your speakers. (by using spacious effects like for instance reverb)

- And between the left speaker and the middle and the right speaker and the middle.

TIP 86

Distortion

Distortion is the alteration of the original shape of something. In our case the waveform. By altering the original shape of a waveform you create musical effects.

I personally use a lot of distortion type effects in my tracks.

A Few examples of how I use distortion:

I place them on inserts just to make sounds come more forward in the mix.

I use distortion to control my levels even more. U can kill the dynamic range for your sound which in some cases is a desirable effect. Like in a comparable way as a compressor.

I use distortion to create completely different sounds. Like making a saw wave lead from a simple bass guitar sample.

I use band distortion to accentuate some frequencie bands of a sound a bit more.

I also use distortion as an FX send. If you like the original sound, don't want to alter it, but you want to add some grittyness you can try it via this way.

I use distortion to create filter sweeps for fills and stuff.

I use bitcrushers to create more presence on your sound

I DON'T use distortion on my masterchannel!

My fav distortion plugin is Quadrafuzz (cubase), Easy, versatile, great sounding.

Breaking down the track

Today I want to talk about an important part of the production process.

Often when I am producing a track I'm usually trying a lot of stuff and creating tons of layers of sounds & beats and placing everything on top of each other until I have reached a creative point where I am happy with it.

And then comes the hard part. Listening!!

What makes the track stand out, what are the key things in your track. Do they stand out?

You need to question yourself again if you really need to double that snare. If you really need to put three fills on top of each other. If you really need all those layers for your lead sound. In the end these things can really clog up your mix and let you forget the important key things of the track.

Start muting stuff and see if you are missing something.

Try to mix that one snare as it would sound when you stack 3.

For me when I'm almost done with a track I usually end up throwing away 30% of the track in the final stage which makes it sound so much tighter again!

Less = More

TIP 88

What is Resonance or Bandpass in a Filter or EQ? What does it do?

Resonance is a boost at the edge of the cut-off frequency. (see upper picture) You can use it to accentuate the frequencies at the cutoff point. In a mix this could be a wise decision just to make it pop out a bit more.

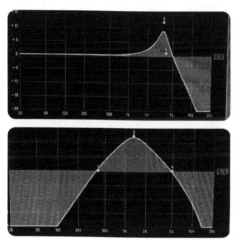

A side effect would be that you create a phaser like effect. Which can be interesting again for sound designing. Think of acid sounds for instance.

However if you want to surgically place a sound in a mix I prefer to use the Bandpass filter. (see lower picture) Then you'll have a low & high frequency cutoff which you can easily sweep from left to right to place it in your mix. This works well with sounds that don't need much space. For instance a top layer of your leads.

Combined with distortion it's also great for sound design. Use it to make that really powerfull lead that fits perfect in your mix.

Try it out, make a sound and switch your filter section between Bandpass filter type or Adding resonance while sweeping the cutoff.
What do you think sounds better?

TIP 89

Mixing In the box or Out of the box?

Analog Summing:

This is a subject which is more or less a matter of taste. It's something on which you can find endless discussions. This is my opinion.

Let me first try and explain in simple words what headroom is.

Let's say if you are mixing a track and that 0 is the floor and 100 is the ceiling. Your mix has to fit in between this.

Then in such a case it would be nice to start your levels at 60 so you would have some room left before you hit the ceiling and unwanted sideeffects start sounding thru your mix like clipping.

In this example 100 would be the ceiling in the digital domain.

But what if you would route it thru an analog summing box? If you do that then you temporarily higher your ceiling to say 140 before bringing it back into the digital domain again. The advantage of this is that you get a much more detailed and wider mix. You really experience more depth in your tracks. And all your elements mix easier into place. Also you can add analog artefacts to your sound which can be desirable. This of course is all dependant on what kind of quality hardware you are using. And also your mixing experience.

Now in dance music we are already so used to the clean "digital/in the box" sound. And that in itself is an effect too. (to my opinion) And of course you can create great mixes in the digital domain. But it never hurts to try and go out of the box. Sometimes that can be just the thing you were looking for!

To use Summing in the best way it's better to do so in the mixing stage. However on mastering level you can hear a clear difference between Digital & Analog.

Workflow:

After you created your awesome melody, it might be a good idea to teach yourself a certain workflow. Cause what 's next? Arranging, mixing, leveling, adding effect, automation? Sometimes it makes sense to work in a specific order. This also helps you to actually finish the track faster and to know when it is finished!

What would be a logic workflow? That probably differs per person. But here's mine:

So after you created your hit melody and groove and most of the creative melody stuff that's gonna make up your track I usually start with the leveling. I usually start with the volume of the Kick and work my way around that., after that I put in the bass to create a great starting point. Then I just follow my routin workflow which most of the time kinda looks like this in a nutshell:

- create the drum groove and mix it in.

- Find an arrangement you want to sort of hang on to

- Build the intro

- Work on the break

- Work on the buildup

- Perfect the buildup

- Make the drop

- Create the transition between drop and 2nd breakdown.

- with every sound you add make sure you cut away all the lowend.

- See where and if effects are needed.

- After this I usually start with the mixdown untill I am satisfied. Use your reference tracks here.

- I accompany the mixdown with automation

- Work on the second break and drop depending on the arrangement you choose ofcourse.

- Make the outro.

- After this you can conclude that the first 90% is done. Which was the easy part

- After that it's tweeking until you are satisfied. Meaning adjusting the mix, cutting of all the tails, Optimize your automation. And testing it on different systems!

- Then if it sounds good and comparable on a quality level with all the other released track out there then you can call it finished!

Of course there can also be certain rules to follow on how to build that intro, break, drop, build up etcetera, but that's a story for another time.

Sub Bassss

Sometimes you really want to tuck away the bass underneath the kick.
I found a very simple solution for that Mixing wise which I accidently
stumbled upon .

Normally you cut off all the highs, maybe even use a Filter add a little
sidechain and some compression.

Besides the sidechain I found a way which works even better for me.
In my example I used the Izotope Dynamics, but you can use any multiband plugin.

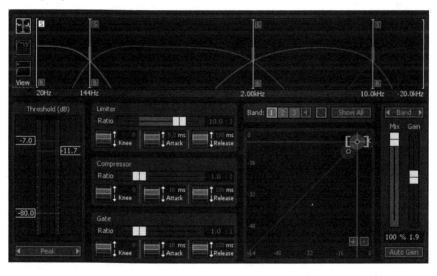

Each plugin would have different characteristics so you would have to try
them out to find the right one for you.

I clicked on the lower band and solo'ed it. I keep it solo'ed and apply some
of the compression as well. Add a little sidechain and adjust volume to
your liking and it will fit in the mix perfectly.

Zero Latency EQ (minimum phase) vs Linear EQ

This is a subject which we can get very technical about. At all, not so interesting actually. So I try to keep this to what you should know.

Every equalizer creates phase shift. The heavier you EQ, the more phase shift you create. If you work with correlated signals like a Multi-Microphone recording or Parallel processing and you start eq-ing one of the two signals you create phase shift between the two which can result in frequency or volume dips/spikes. That's something you want to avoid. So in that case I would recommend using a Linear EQ. Cause this makes sure that there occurs no phase shift.

Also when you are making dramatic EQ processes it is smart to switch to Linear from time to time to hear what the difference is. Heavy EQ'ing equals bigger phaseshifts. So in Linear you might get better results.

In linear EQ Mode you get a latency which is compensated by default in your DAW. If you would use a Linear EQ on your kickdrum for instance you would notice less transient. Be Aware of that. That same latency can also be used in your advantage to "smear" your mix a bit more.

EQ'ing Reverbs & Delays

Always try to EQ your reverbs & delays. Put your reverb on a very high level, take a boosted bell EQ and sweep your frequency spectrum. There where it sounds the most annoying you start cutting the frequencies there. Now listen to what a difference that makes in your whole mix. You still have to hear the reverb of course but other instruments in that frequency spectrum should sound more clearer now.

TIP 94

Sampling & Restoring Old Samples

Sometimes it's really cool to use an old sample in your track. But the quality can be really shit.
The most common things you'll find are the side effects from old vinyl records.
To get those sampled parts back to the standards of nowaday you can try a few things.
I personally always use these four plugins from Waves (X-Click, X-Crackle, X-Hum, X-noise). You have some even more specialized software for restauration like Izotope RX.

Waves X-click tries to suppress clicks and spikes from transients.

X-crackle suppresses the crackles you hear on vinyl disks.
X-hum filters out specific frequencies with linked notch filters to clean up your audio. Usually especially in the lower end.
X-noise suppresses the noisefloor sounds from old analog equipment. It also helps to just mute the audio parts in between the waveforms.

After this you can normalize your sample to get the volume to a normal level and EQ and compress as normal.

Sometimes there is one specific click in your sample which you want to let disappear.
In Wavelab you'll find a special pencil tool with which you can redraw the waveform.

Furthermore it can help to apply a little room reverb and delay on the sample. This also helps to mask some of the imperfections of the older sample.

If all else fails it helps to double your old sample with a recreated sample you made.

That: "What The Fuck Just Happened Moment!"

Sometimes you experience things in your career as a producer that leave you flabbergasted for life. It is how you deal with those moments in your career that will define you as an artist/dj/businessman.

Let me tell you a story......................(dreamclouds, fade outtt....)

It's January, snow is falling and you locked yourself up in your studio. After a month of hard work in the studio you finally made that one song which you are sure that the big labels will sign. You even wrote the lyrics for this one. You hired a friend who sang the demo for 200 Dollars. You say demo but it actually sounds so good it can be released as is.
Since 4 months you have a manager. You send your demo over to your manager and try to let him find a big label.

Labels don't always respond that fast so after a Month you ask your manager to send a reminder. 3 weeks later finally a response from a big label that they love the record!!!
Your pre-party starts right away. Champagne popping cause it's finally going to happen.
After a week you receive the contract from the recordcompany which is full of language you don't understand and care about, but hey you have a manager who will take care of it.
You receive his phonecall and he tells you that the label wants to sign an exclusive deal with you. Hapinness doesn't stop for you and you sign that deal right away.

After a week you receive a phonecall from there A&R saying that they wanna resing the track cause they have doubts about the vocal.
The recordcompany sends the track out to some of it's writers and another month passes.
It's now June when your demo gets send back with a new awesome vocal on it.

Wow, you never imagined that this would happen. It sounds even better now. It was really worth the wait. Although you loose 50% of the copyrights and some royalties.

Your recordlabel is in Las Vegas during EDC and the EDMBizz conference. They play the new demo to a major record label.
After a week you receive a phonecall that a major label is interested in the track and they want to feature it with one of there major artists... OMFG, really!!

The major artist wants to re-write a couple of the lyrics and play an extra guitarline on top. You don't even care cause you know this will be straight fire when it gets released!
It's August and you receive the new version with the Big Feature on it.

The major label wants to send it out to the engineer for mixing and after that to mastering. That will cost an extra 6500 Dollar ,but hey that will earn itself back real fast.
It's the end of September and the Track is finally finished.
You start asking for a release date and they are telling you that it's somewhere near the end of April next year.

Oooh, that's long..
The next week you get a phone call from your manager. He's trying to figure out how to deal with the contract which is now between, You / The label / The Major Label / The featured artist and his Laywers. Splits have to be made. And you end up with a 8% copyright split and a 1% producers royalty. All costs for mixing, mastering, video, remixes, promo can be deducted from your royalty. And you have to waive your rights for at least two big commercials and a Movie. (meaning you don't get paid for the use of your music)
Also they want the major artist name first.
But they are willing to give you a 30K Advance on release which is more then enough to buy that car youwant and to finally make some adjustments to your studio.

After a good nights sleep you realize it isn't all fair but this shit is now going on for 8 Months already and you just want it to be released, so you give in and sign the contract.

A new winter has passed and it's March. More then a year later!!

You get really excited cause it's almost releasetime. You ask your manager and label for an update which after a week you get.

"Dear Label and Artist,
we have signed a new album deal with our major artist and we have decided that your single doesn't fit his new direction. We therefor decided to end the agreement, effective immediately."

Wait what?!

Totally flabbergasted you stay in your bed for a week deciding how you can ever tell your friends and family what happened. Fuck you already put out an option on that new car..
Another Month passes..
It's April now and you fantasize about how it would have been if the track was released.

But then it hits you!
You could always release the older version without the feature on it. Just take out the old version and release that..
You ask your manager to set it up for you.
It takes a few weeks to get a reply.

"Dear Artist,

After carefull debate we have decided that we find the track to outdated.
We therefor decided not to release this track.
Please keep us in mind if you have something else"

Best Regards,

Performance

So the last couple of weeks my (old) pc couldn't handle my projects anymore.
My VST Performance started to max out. And before I finally received my new computer I had to boost my old one just keep the current projects active without having to bounce out everything everytime.

The last week was all about installing my new PC, which was extremely boring and annoying to do. But now I have a real beast.

But since it was so boring I decided to do a boring tip about boosting your PC performance.

We all know the common things like:

- Turn of programs you don't need that are running in the background

- Defrag your disk

- Turn of powersave

- Etcetera.

But there was one i did not know off which also helped really good.
And that's to make some adjustments in the processor power management:
Enable Maximum Performance Power Settings
Step 1
Click Start, "Control Panel" and then "Power Options."
Step 2
Click the "Show Additional Plans" drop-down arrow. Enable the "High Performance" option then click "Change Plan Settings."
Step 3
Click the "Change Advanced Power Settings" link in the new window. The Power Options window appears.
Step 4

Click the "+" symbol next to the "Processor Power Management" value, then "Minimum Processor State." Click the "Setting %" label, then change the value in the box field to "100."

Step 5

Click "System Cooling Policy" then the "Setting" label. Change the value to "Active."

Step 6

Click "Maximum Processor State" then "Setting." Change the value to "100."

Step 7

Click the "Apply" button then "OK." Click the "back" arrow button in the Edit Plan Settings window. Close the Select a Power Plan window. Windows applies the changes to the power settings and utilizes 100 percent of the processor available power for the active application on the screen.

Increase CPU Usage Priority for an Application

Step 1

Launch the application for which you want to increase the CPU usage priority in Windows.

Step 2

Right-click the Windows taskbar then click "Start Windows Task Manager."

Step 3

Click the "Applications" tab in the Windows Task Manager window. Right-click the application name, then click "Go to Process." The Process tab opens with the process for the application highlighted.

Step 4

Right-click the highlighted process, then click "Set Priority." Choose "Real Time" on the pop-up list.

Step 5

Close the Windows Task Manager window. After you set the priority for an application to "Real Time," Windows will use as much available CPU power as possible for the selected program even if you minimize it to the taskbar and make active another program window.

Match EQ

A Match EQ is an equalizer that allows you to analyze the spectral content of your reference track towards your own mix and apply the difference to your mixdown.

So let's say you are a great fan of the mixdown of a certain track. Cause it has a great low end and a superclear high end for instance.

In that case you would take a snapshot (or analyze) the average frequency spectrum of that track. After takin that snapshot you would take a snapshot of your own mix and then you let the computer calculate what the difference is between your track and the reference track.

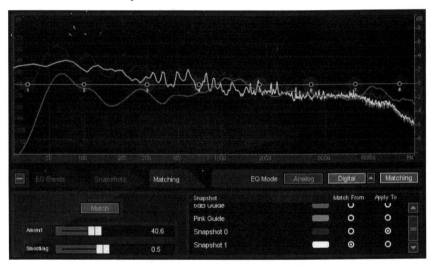

After that you can mix in the EQ changes to your own mix to match your reference track.

You can also apply this on stems only of course.

TIP 98

Reverb

A nice way to set up a reverb signal is by applying a Mid/Side EQ on the send channel after the reverb.

Here you can cut away some of the mid information. While boosting a bit of the sides to create an even wider sound.

To top things off you can apply a little bit of sidechain effect to make it a bit tighter.

TIP 99

Back To Basics

There is an important rule in mixing that I can't stress enough.

To make a mix sound good you actually only need

- Leveling (volumes)

- EQ (Seperation of frequencies)

- Compressor (for gluing and Headroom control)

- Reverb (for placement and depth control)

- Delay (for placement and depth control)

If you master these 5 trades you can mix any track.

To learn this try to stick to one EQ, Compressor and FX for a while. It doesn't really matter which brand they are.

If you use the same things very often then you will know exactly what each knob adjustments will do to your sound.

After you master that you can use different Eq's and Compressors and then you will start to hear differences between them. Only then you can use those differences to your advantage.

TIP 100

Making the 808

So I'm currently working on a track which needed a nice 808 sound. I'm sure there are million ways to make one. But this is one of them.

First you start with finding that kick which has the right Attack which you wanna hear. Could be a Tom, Dubstep kick, 808 kick or a combination of those, whatever.
But this is also what gives it some character.

You trim/shorten that sample down until you have only the attack/ short decay left.
You cut away a bit of the low end +/- 95hz in my case.
Then you gonna find your subbas. I'm using Serum for this one.
I found a nice Subbas and applied a pitch envelope. So you really feel the subkick is gliding a bit down in pitch every time you play a note.

Now if you put the attack kick and the sub kick on top of each other they propably don't sit perfect in your mix.

So you can set a sidechain compressor on your subbas and sidechain it with a copied track of the Attack kick. That way the sub will duck whenever the attack is being played, so you will always hear a clean attack on the kick.
Now to get it even better you can play around with the attack envelope of the Subbass and put that a little less tighter.
Afer this EQ the sub and compress it in a way that the volume stays in place. Add distortion via insert or a send to your liking.

A Musical Formula....

So here's a little Music theory for Starters and Noobs (like me). If you are already familiar with music theory skip to the next tip.

For all others, this can really help you out if you are writing melodies.

A Few BASIC rules:
There are 8 notes in a scale! The C-scale is the easiest to learn cause it has no flats and no sharps. It consists of the pitches C, D, E, F, G, A, B and C

How to make a triad chord (three notes at once) from a scale.

C-Scale (triad) looks like this. (I'm ONLY using the basic 6 chords here)

Mjr mn mn Mjr Mjr mn
1 2 3 4 5 6
C D E F G A
E F G A B C
G A B C D E

First chord = C/E/G, second chord = D/F/A, 3rd chord – E/G/B and so one.

Now for how to play them you could use a handy tool which you should try out. So the numbers hereunder correspond with the numbers I put in the C-scale above. And then just follow these steps:

1 > goes to any
2 > goes to 5
3 > goes to 6
4 > goes to 1 or 5
5 > goes to 1
6 > goes to 2

Example: You start with the 1 chord (C,E,G), then you decide to play number 6 (A,C,E). These steps tell you to go from 6 to number 2, so you play

(D,F,A), from 2 you go to number 5 (G,B,D) and 5 goes back to number 1 and the perfect loop is complete.

And cause the C-scale is the easiest to learn cause it has no flats and sharps, you can play whatever white key melody on your piano on top of those chords and it will sound great.

Now if you have made a great melody in the C-scale you can easily transpose it to a different Scale-Key.

You can apply this to every scale in the same way.
Try it, you feel like an instant musician....

TIP 102

How to create a big lead!?

Let's say you are creating a big lead. You want it to sound very big (spatial) so you decide to put a reverb on it.

Now a cool way to use that reverb is to put a sidechain compressor after the reverb insert.

And then you sidechain the Compressor to the exact same melody which you are playing with your big Lead.

This way the reverb ducks on the attacks of the Lead sound making sure it cuts even better thru your mix while keeping it spatial.

Lowpass

When you are cutting away the high end of a stem with a lowpass filter to create more headroom, it will also help if you give a boost to the cutoff frequency. This way you compensate a bit for the loss in high frequencies. And you also create a point where that particular sound will cut thru your mix.

Example:
Green = the cutoff filter
Blue = the compensation for the loss
Yellow = the point where it will cut thru your mix

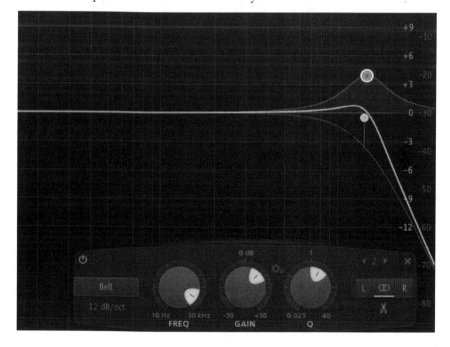

TIP 104

Business Tip

When something looks to good to be true it probably is.

As a beginning DJ you are always scouting for some gigs. And a lot of promoters / clubowners will tell you :

"If you play for free tonight and you do well then I will pay you for your next booking".

As this may look like a great opportunity for you, you might sell yourself short. It's always better to let the promoter pay for the booking and if he's happy afterwards then you can offer a discount for the next gig.

TIP 105

Sampling, a few ins and outs you might not now

So last week I reposted something about 'Drake' and the amount of samples that are used in his tracks.
I personally don't mind sampling. But if it's recognizable as a sample then it needs to be cleared with the original artist.
Which I'm pretty sure they did for Drake's album.

Why do you sample?
It usually adds a particular feeling to a track which you just can't recreate yourself.

The most sampled track of all time must be James Brown – Funky Drummer. That breakbeat is used in countless tracks. But never cleared.

And the artist who is absolute creative best at sampling has got to be the prodigy:
(Check out : The making of The Prodigy – Smack My Bitch up in Ableton on Youtube)

So when you make a track there are 2 main ways of income.

The Sales royalties (meant for artist, producer, laywers) which we can call the 'Master' part.
and the Mechanical/Performance royalties (meant for writers, producers and artist) which we can call the 'Publishing'.

Now if you would sample something,
you need to clear "The master" and you need the clear the "Publishing" of that sample.
Meaning that artist from the sample will be on the credits as a producer/artist and as a writer.
Now If you would cover (Replay/Resing) the sample it's not always necessary to clear the master. That depends on the country your in and which

countries will be releasing that track. In Holland for instance you can cover any song.

It's always wise to contact a publisher who can help you with this. So you don't get sued afterwards.

Nowadays producers make a lot of bootlegs which they PROMOTE as a free download in exchange for Facebook likes or whatever.
It's very debatable if this can be seen as a breach of rights or not.
Some laywers see openings to stop these 'Free Releases' and even claim compensation.
So beware.

TIP 106

Vocals

This is a great Tip I got from "The voice of Hardstyle" himself, Harald Bruijstens.

I asked him if he has a specific routine for when he is recording his vocals. These are some of his tips to get that quality vocal.

Make sure you practiced the stuff before you record it. Lot of people tend to record a lot of loops and then take the usable parts out of all the takes. It's better to prepare and record and then make a selecting from only good takes.

Make sure your input is good. Good input equals good output. Meaning right recording volume, good mic, warmed up voice etc..

After recording, first start to delete all the puffs and ticks and noises. If you need to de-ess, do it manually. That way you have better control. Use volume dips or crossfade techniques.

If necessary correct some of the pitches that went wrong in Melodyne or Vari-audio.

Send the recorded vocal(s) to a bus.

Then first the Compressor.
Then Eq, to accentuate the high
Then a reverb on send or Insert. Whatever you prefer.
Then a parallel compression to taste (see former tips about that)

In essence this should be enough to create a good quality vocal.

Creating more impact on the drop

An easy way to give a drop just a bit more impact is to make a Downwards volume fade with your master or group channels in the build-up. Combine that with an upwards spatial and Highpass fade and it will kick in even harder.

The Waveshaper

With a waveshaper you can custom shape the waveform of your sound. By changing the waveform you create a distortion of the waveform, which in return creates a cool effect.

I use it for distortion effects. Particularly for sounddesign purposes. But sometimes also as a replacement for a compressor and distortion unit. Just to let a sound cut better thru your mix. Distortion keeps the levels of your signal steady and kills your dynamics. Which can be usefull if used right.

It's also nice to put it in as a send (aux) to mix in some harshness where needed.

A simple but effective plugin for this is the CM Waveshaper.

Phase and Mono questions

So every week I get a lot of questions about phase problems and mono compatibility.
We have discussed this already back in Tip 37, 50 & 51.

But here are a few extra tips:

- Always check your mix in Mono often during mixdown. This way you can find and fix problems faster.

- How to make that synth fatter with detune without loosing mono compatibility? If you have an oscillator with multiple voices and they are detuned. Try to add an extra oscillator with just one voice or not detuned at all. And make sure that oscillator is harder in volume then the detuned one. This way the volume will stay more up when played in mono.

- The more elements you mix in Mono, the wider a stereo mixed lead will sound. Don't overdue your stereo imagers.

- Some synthesizers let you pan the oscillators. Let's say you build a sound, pan one osc towards the left, one to the right and one in the middle. And you make sure the middle one has the loudest volume. It will still sound good in Mono.

- Some daws have "invert polarity/phase" switches. This may create a sonic difference if your signals are out of phase.

- Sometimes it's just usefull to only create superwide reverbs. Then when you 'mono' your mix it will sound super tight and when it's back in stereo it feels wide.

How to keep your delays tight

When you are working with vocals or melody and you are putting a delay on it. It can be a good thing to do automation on your feedback time. Increase the feedback when there's space between the notes or words and decrease when melodies get faster. This way you create a much tighter mix.

Reverb / Mono

We already discussed some of the advantages of mixing in Mono. Tweaking your reverb settings is also easier to do in Mono. This way you will hear better if you are using to much or to little reverb and if it sounds to muddy in your mix.

When it sounds good in Mono it will sound even better in Stereo.

TIP 112

Kick vs Bass

A nice way to start balancing/ mixing the kick to the bass is to find the frequency of the bassnote. (See tip 45 for which Key corresponds with what frequency). Let's say your bass is in F, that corresponds with 87Hz. Now take your equalizer and Boost your kick a few dB at 87Hz with a High Q. And attenuate your bass a few dB at 87 Hz with a high Q. You will notice that it starts to blend much better together.

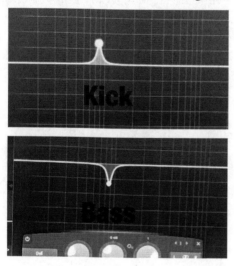

Production Tip: "The Sampler"

Every DAW has his own sampler. And they all have slightly different functions then in the other DAW's. (So there are many options to this)

But in Basic, this is a cool production tip which you can start with right away.

Take a sample, any sample. Now timestretch it longer to a point that it still sounds ok and not to granulized. In time you will notice which type of samples work better and which not. Now, figure out the key of that sample.

Import that audiofile into your sampler. Since you have stretched the file it gives you a bit more key scale and longer notes to play with.

Add to your liking: the monophonic, legato, glide, portamento switch. Depending on your DAW and start messing around.

Add a pitchbend +24 and you can start scratching with the sample too.

This way you'll get creative really fast and make sounds that no one else has.

TIP 114

FX chain experimenting

Usually all the tips that I write find their origin from something I had to deal with on that same day. So today I was mixing in some 'Groovy Horns'. But they didn't fill the spectrum in a way I wanted to.

So I made one fx (Auxiliary) bus and placed some reverb and a delay on it and
Also a stereowidener.
And to top it of I added two volume sidechain plugins on top of that too. (lfo tool, kickstart, whatever). Too really exaggerate the pumping effect.

So I mixed that effect in with the original Horns and they suddenly came alive.

Now you still have a clear sound in the front but a lot of energetic action going on in the background and the sides.

This was exactly what I was looking for .

Try it on your lead sound and see what happens.

Thicken up your vocals & Lead

So this week an interesting tip on how to thicken up your vocal or leads without using any vst's.

Just a formula.

Now I found this formula somewhere online and tried to replicate it and it sounds very good.

What you want to do is as follows. Bounce your lead/vocal to audio.

Name it "Lead" track.

Now copy this same track 8 times over and put those in a folder for your convenience. Pan track 1,3,5,7 Hard Left. And 2,4,6,8 Hard Right.

For each track it should be possible to fill in a delay time in milliseconds. (usually in the inspector window). And it should also be possible to tune your tracks in cents rather then full notes.

Now set the following delays and tunings for your tracks:

L1, 10 ms, -3 Cents   R1, 24 ms +3 cents

L2, 24 ms, +6 Cents   R2, 10 ms, -6 Cents

L3, 10 ms, -9 Cents   R3, 24 ms, +9 Cents

L4, 24 ms, +12 Cents   R4, 10 ms, -12 Cents

See photo.

If a track delay is below 10 Milliseconds you will not really notice it. If you make the delay time longer then 30 Milliseconds you will notice to much phasing. So keep those times between 10 & 30.

Also if you would mix in these 8 tracks to hard you will notice some bad side effects too. So mix it in gentle.

Now send those 8 tracks to a group bus and gently mix them in with your "Lead Track" and check out the results.

TIP 116

Sometimes tiny differences matter in the final endresult

I briefly mentioned this tip ones before. But I was using it a lot this week while mixing that I wanted to point it out again.

If you are mixing a track and want to push out a certain elements in the mix a bit more. In my case I wanted the bassline and 2 leads to stand out more from the rest.

A great way for doing that is to put a tube distortion in an FX send (Aux,bus). Also add an eq after that and cut off everything above 14 kHz or so. Now gently mix in some of that distorted signal with the original signal. This is a great way to add a bit more power to that sound and in the Mid section in general. An additional benefit would be that the sounds you put it on will become a bit more cohesive. As long as you don't overdo it of course.

How to use the solo button?!

It all sounds so easy. If you are mixing, you solo a sound. You Eq and compress it until it sounds good and voila.

But this is actually not the right way to go. Cause this way for example your synth lead may not work with your bass.
Or you just create problems cause your mixing everything in the same frequency span.

I use the Solo button in 'producer' mode. So if I'm adding a certain melody, deleting ticks, creating fade-ins and outs or creating an extra fill or fx I usually solo, then create the event, unsolo and then try to mix it in with the rest.
I also mix while I am producing the track.
To me personally that's the same thing.
But I know lots of people that first produce a song and then start mixing.

I also use Solo in group or folder mode.
Folders for example to listen to the full beat as a whole.
Or group mode when I wanna check if my group sounds cohesive enough.

The great advantages about mixing in an unsolo'd environment is of course that you are always concentrating on the complete mix. You learn to listen even better.
Individual sounds may sound thin or strange but in the whole mix they sound great cause the elements complement each other.

So try and loop a part that you are mixing. And try to eq and balance that one sound while everything is playing. And then just walk thru your track this way.
It takes some getting used to, but in the end your mixdown will happen much faster with better results.

TIP 118

Grouping

Grouping is when you send several tracks to one Bus (channel, fader).

This can come in handy for a lot of purposes. For instance

- Putting a multitrack recording under one fader.

- If you want to use one specific effect on several tracks. For instance a sidechain plugin. Route all channels to the group and apply the effect.

- To create a better overview in your daw.

- Gain staging (from channel mix, to group mix, to masterfader)

There is one other specific use for grouping which I normally use a lot.

If you work with sounds that are similar to each other. Like 2 or 3 basslines. Or three layers of synths or all your drums. In that case I would mix each channel seperately so that they already sound good before sending it to a group. And then in the group I would put a compressor or similar insert to blend all the sounds a bit more together. So you get that compact sound.

Quantize / Swing

The possibility to put your rhytm just off the grid to create a swinging movement.

In most DAW's and hardware drummachines you can find a quantization or swing functions.

This swing already was used in the 1930's in Jazz songs and is since then used in all sorts of music with of course hip hop also as a major user of the swing functions in the MPC machines.

When we look at dance music it has also played a huge role in the creation of house/disco type grooves. And to my opinion techno is just one big swing pattern.

You can apply it to everything. Drums, Synths, basslines etc..

I prefer using it on drums, (snares particularly) or when I use a sample. Let it be a vocal loop, a disco loop, a drumbeat. I like to cut that up in 16th or 8th notes and apply some quantization on that. Just to create your own groove with that sample.

From a listeners point of view it will be more pleasing to listen to and makes it more dance able. And from a mixing point of view you create a little bit more space for your shorter elements. Although if you apply to much it can cause phase too.

The absolute easiest way to start using swing within your DAW is to put a note on every 16th. Quantize them straight to begin with. Then apply your groove / swing and listen to what happens. After that you start deleting notes to create your own rhytm.

In drumcomputers, hardware or software you can apply it to whole groups at once. Start experimenting with it and see what you can do with it.

The importance of recognizable Loops

Your standing in the club, the dj is mixing in a new track, you already recognize the intro so you know which track is coming.

A good drumloop could create so much recognition that it is a super important part of your track. I mean everybody recognizes Michael Jackson – Billy Jean from the first second.

It's the groove and the choice of drums and additional sounds that should make you able to listen to the loop for hours, without it ever getting bored.

So don't just take a Kick, Snare and Clap. But try to let them stand out. Make them your own. Apply weird effects like phaser, flangers and non-typical delays, different EQ settings just to experiment.

That's why a lot of people sampled from the catchy 70's Disco Tracks and used them for their house productions. Back in the day ('95) I always went to the library in Rotterdam where you could lent Sample cd's full of those loops. I chopped those up, combined them and tried to make them even more catchier.

I released a Spire soundset. For the people who buy this they will receive a small sample cd (around 200+ samples) as a bonus with around 60 of those iconic loops. Which are just waiting to be re-used again.

I also added some oldschool sounds. Incl my old kicks from back in the Jumpstyle era.

But also the Kicks that I have used in the past few years and still using.

Groove Extraction

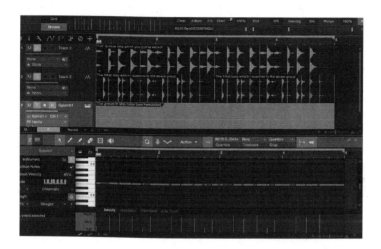

Did you know that it is possible to extract the groove from every audio loop? So imagine pulling in an audio loop of this amazing groovy bassline. By quantizing it to the groove it will place markers at every attackpoint in the audiofile. (see picture) This groove can be extracted to either a midi file so in that case you can use your own sounds instead. But also you can save the quantized groove as a preset and apply it other audiofiles you are using in the track, so that everything would sound supertight. This was done in Studio One. But you should be able to do this in every DAW.

Melodies

I always get a lot of questions about how you make a catchy melody. It's a bit of a weird question but there is actually a way to tackle this.

First find a sound which sounds different, catchy and fat. This will take most of your time ;-).

Then start with the "one finger melody"

Create a melody that you can play with one finger. Make sure it loops well and that it doesn't get bored after playing it for a while.

Then start finding the chords which you can play underneath it.

After that find the bassline which you can play underneath. You can extract that from the chords. But it's always nice if it follows a slightly different path then the notes of the chords.

After this you have a good basis for the melody. Now complement it with a counter melody, a bridge melody and some random chord stabs and your done

TIP 123

Serial compression trick

So there is this theory that if you want more loudness in your end mix it's better to apply more then 1 compressor after each other.

Instead of just putting one compressor on the masterbus you apply more. With each compressor doing a tiny bit of gain reduction instead of one big gain reduction.
That way you even out the peaks smoother which results in your mix sounding more natural, more dynamic and louder.

How to create more impact on your drop

A great way of creating a bit more impact on your drop is to make sure that that part of the song is 1 or 2 dB louder then the rest.

You could automate your master fader for that by either boosting the drop part or by decreasing the volume of the rest of your song.

Or by automating one of the volume / gain knobs on your mastering plugin.

If you would combine this with Tip 107 you create the maximum impact.

Wall of sound

Today I wanna talk about the **'Wall Of Sound'** in combination with layering.

The previous tips (16, 53, 73) gave you a good start with layering.

But I want to elaborate some more on the subject.
In order to create a full sound you have to think 3 dimensional.

You can place stuff in the middle or at the sides of your mix.
You can place stuff in front of you or in the back of your mix.
And you can place stuff high and low in your mix.

Now if you look at this picture, you see I made a lead consist out of 4 sounds.

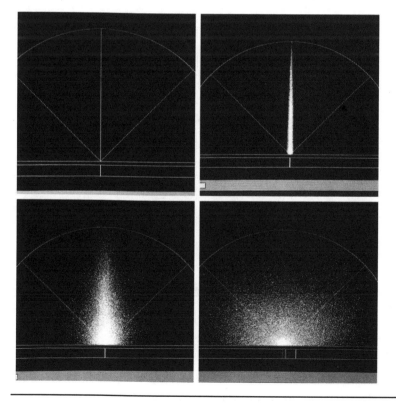

One is straight in the middle and dry, So it feels upfront and is fully mono. The second one is also straight in the midde but you can see that there is some fx on it (reverb, delay, distortion) cause it scatters a bit. So it sounds a little bit more to the back and a little bit wider.

The third one is already more panned and also some fx on it. So it's less mono compatible, feels wider and slightly more to the back of your mix. The fourth is just superwide. Fully panned, stereowidening applied, not mono compatible. All the information is towards the sides.

So combine these four, which don't necessarily need to play the exact same melody. Meaning for instance the Chords in the middle, Upper melodies towards the sides.

Now face your head towards the speaker and you will notice that you will have a wide and deep sound from Left to Right and from the Front towards the Back.

Which if you press the mono button would still be standing strong in your mix.

TIP 126

Motivation

Building your career as a DJ/Producer can be a long journey full of ups and downs.

But as long as you stay true to yourself you can always look back and into the future with a sense of pride and dignity.

Don't be jealous of other peoples 'success' since that wil only distract you from reaching your own goals. Success is only relative.

Learn from people that inspire you, don't copy what they are doing.

Social media can create a lot of envy and pressure amongst DJ's and Producers (anybody actually)

Most of it is special social media created moments anyway. Letting you think of connections that aren't actually there.

Things usually look better then they really are.

Except for Aruba of course. lol

You need to realize for yourself what is important to you and stay on that path.

Then you will find true success and all that comes along with it!

Limiting & Transients

This week a tip which sometimes leads to interesting results.

If you are limiting your group bus channel and feel that you are loosing a lot of transients, you could place a transient designer before the limiter and exaggerate the transients before they pass thru the limiter.

Hereby you could compensate the loss of transients AND still keep the same amount of headroom.

Try it in your mix and see which results you get.

TIP 128

EQ Automation

This is an easy Tip most people tend to forget.

Example:

Let's say you have a main sound in your drop and in the second part of the drop you'll add another synth on top which conflicts a bit with the main sound. To fix this you could automate the EQ of the main sound to fit better with the added synth but only for that part of the song. This way the two sounds blend a bit better without loosing any energy. You could also apply this very conveniently to Synths vs Vocals. For instance cut away a little bit of the midrange of the synths, only when the vocal is also playing.

TIP 129

Mixing with a spectrum analyzer

There are some things you are not supposed to be doing while mixing and that is peaking to much at the Spectrum Analyzer.
So automatically we go check the Analyzer as often as we can.
A spectrum analyzer can give you information on a certain piece of audio.
As you see here on the photo is a spectrum analysis of a vocal.

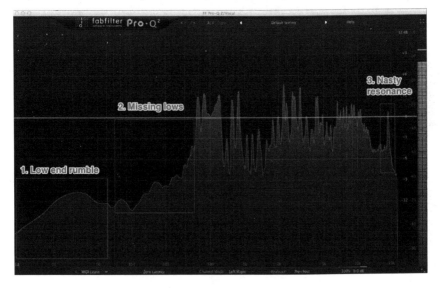

You can clearly tell that it is lacking some body around 250 Hz. You can also tell it's lacking some presence between 1 & 2 Khz.

You can also apply a spectrum analyzer on your master. Try to find a reference track in the same style and preferably the same Key as well. As that makes it easier to compare. It's hard to say what a well balanced curve for your master should be. But for a more bass orientated track (Dance music in general) this should be a nice reference curve for your master. see photo 2

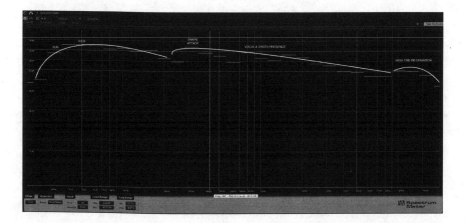

Now if all the spectrum curves look great that is still not a garantuee that your track will sound great. So keep using your ears.

The more you are used to your own studio room while side-looking to your spectrum meters on individual sounds, the more you will be able to use them in a good way.

Try to reference some known tracks thru the spectrum analyzer and see how they compare with each other.

TIP 130

The Expander

So here is a plugin that most people don't use that often but surely need to try it out.

In the NON-EDM world expanders are mostly used to help suppress noise or bleed from live recordings. This is called a downward expander.

It behaves very similarly to a gate, except that it's not a simple on/off type of process but it works with a ratio.

In the EDM world you can use downward expanders to create tighter loops. Or to reduce the noise in a sample you took from an old record for instance. On the other hand nowadays people use a lot of guitar in dance tracks. And a downward expander can seriously help you to get control over the applied distortion.

But they can also be used to increase the dynamic range of a signal.

This is called an upward expander. Let's say you have a piece of audio that is compressed completely flat and you want to make it sound a bit more lively you could apply an upward expander which increases the range between the softest en the loudest peaks again by multiplying the output by the ratio you have set.

TIP 131

Blockchain

Today somewhat more of a different education.
I'm currently dealing with a lot of contractual bullshit and a lawsuit while making new music, prepping interviews etc...
I hear you thinking :"So what?, all in a days work, right?"

Well, yes that's true!

But today it irritated a bit more then usual. So that is why today I would like to point out this new piece of technology that is popping up slowly and is going to revolutionize a lot of industries including the music industry. This technology is called blockchain.

"In the music industry, the blockchain could transform publishing, monetization and the relationship of artists with their communities of fans."

All the information of a track is stored in a blockchain. It can validate and register transactions without the need of a central authority like a publisher or recordcompany or a downloadportal like beatport.
This technology will eventually make payments direct to the artist; Without waiting 2 years for it, without transfer costs and completely cutting out the middle man so most of the revenue will actually end up for the artist. Instead of the crums. Wooow!

A few artist are pioneering this new technology.
As for instance DJ hardwell recently did.
I foresee a future where artists can hold all their master- and copyrights. And where the traditional record company is a thing of the past.

Now this all sounds to good to be true and I'm sure a few hurdles must be taken for it to work properly.

TIP 132

'Magic'

The Practical Approach

So today I have an assignment for all producers out there.

1.   Start a new project.

2.   Put your end buss in MONO right away. (important, don't forget!)

3.   Now go look for your polyphonic Lead synth you want to use.

4.   Play and record your melody.

5.   Open up your EQ and cut away all the LowEnd untill +/- 100Hz.

6.   Open up an Izotope mastering plugin (or similar)

7.   Go to the harmonic exciter and add some in the High-Mid and Highs

8.   Go to the stereo-imaging and add some in the High-Mid and Highs

9.   You won't hear the stereo imaging cause you are still in Mono

10.   Put your master in Stereo again and Voila!

Thank me later

TIP 133

Pre-Delay

This is a tip which with some small tweaks can make a big difference in the perception of your total mixdown.

The pre-delay on your reverb sets the time between the dry signal and the start of the reverb signal. (Early reflections)

If you would set your pre-delays a bit later, the dry sound would punch better thru your mix. Which results in a tighter and clearer mix.

TIP 134

The best way to get a loud mix!

I personally find this pretty difficult. But try to mix your track at low monitoring levels. I must say, The bigger your speakers the easier that is.

It forces you to create energy and excitement when loud volume is not an option.

You will be more considerate when using the EQ and Compressor and also the leveling of the faders and the soundplacements will be done more accurately.

If it sounds big at low levels it will sound even better at loud club volume.

Boosting the Low end - An easy guide

Use only one bass sound as your main low-end source.
High-pass the other 'Bass Sounds' at around 100Hz.
This way you avoid phase problems in the low end.

The low end of your mix will stress your level meters the most. So if you only use one main low -end source and make sure that it has no abnormal peaks (by compressing it) then you can really increase the low end levels even more. And it will result in a louder mix as a whole as well.

TIP 136

"Making a hit is easier then collecting the money for it."

This is a quote I immortalized in a stone tile a long time ago. (bathroom wall decorations)

For everybody that is producing from his bedroom and hoping that one day you can live from your music you need to understand this subject and know that this can make a big difference for your career.

I recently came across a very interesting article written by the Ceo/ Founder of TuneCore – Jeff Price about what happens with your publishing royalties.
I URGE you to read this. No matter if you are a seasoned veteran or a beginning producer. This is something you need to understand.

http://www.hypebot.com/...the-global-songwriter-shell-game-w...

Now this article focusses mainly on digital downloads and streams. But just for fun let me give you another example with pshysical sales.

This year a track of mine got on an album in Japan which sold more then 250.000 CD copies.
Let's try and calculate the publishing I would earn from this cd alone and how much got deducted along the way:

So 250.000 Copies are sold.
30 Dollar is the average price for the cd = 7.500.000 Dollar total sales
9% (average) is paid for the Mechanical royalty = 675.000 Dollar

Divide that by 22 Tracks = 30681,81 Dollar per Track.

JASRAC = Japanese collecting agency takes 15% admin fee

That leaves us with 26.079,54

I have a 40% Share in this track which leaves me with 10431,- Dollar

I have a subpublisher in Japan who collects the money from JASRAC which takes 10%.

Leaves me with 9387,90

I have a publisher in Holland who chases and administeres these money streams. They charge 33%.
Which leaves me with 6261,72 Dollar.

I pay a 5% admin fee to Stemra which leaves me with 5948,64 Dollar

Of the 33% I get back 50% (called a kickback) but of course there is a 10% admin fee for that kickback. So that leaves me with 1411,- Dollar.

Making a total of: 7359,64 Dollar = 1,09% of the total amount.
In this calculation I will leave the bank transfer costs, the currency conversion (Yen to Dollars to Euro) ,the taxes and all other unforseen hidden costs out of the equation.

The total costs you paid behind the scenes to get your 7359,64 Dollar are a total of
8923,63 Dollar.
And the average waiting time to get this money in your bank account is approximately two years.

Now as you can read in the article the splits for the US could be even more unfavorable and for digital exploitation (downloads, streams) things are a bit worse actually.

In this day and age when everything can be digitalized it should be easily feasible to let the digital music services pay out your mechanical royalties. But instead we have to deal with a complex copyright law, the total lack of transparency by the collection agencies and the inability to audit anything. This creates the perfect storm for global copyright infringement with hundreds of millions of dollars of other people's money getting siphoned off and/or not paid to the millions of rightful copyright holders."

TIP 137

Layering

If you layer a lot of kicks or snares/claps on top of each other to create your own personal kick/snare/clap it's better to bounce those stems back to one sample and reimport that one sample.

I've always found that it sounds just a bit better in your mix. Not sure why. And

The bouncing of layered stems also cleans up your mix view.

Same thing goes for midi stuff. If you have layered three synths which play the same melody. Bounce them DRY to audio and process them when it's one audio stem. It gives you more control and they will sound tighter.

TIP 138

Squeezing out that final bit of extra loudness

So your mix is all set and done. It already sounds good, but you want to see if it's possible to squeeze out a little more loudness.

So as your very final plugin on your masterbuss you place a Maximizer. In other words; A Brickwall limiter with an automatic gain function attached to the threshold. Let me stress out that I use this only for just a tiny bit. Don't go over the top with this..

There are several good ones out there. But for the mastering of my latest track I compared the following two.

The L3 Multimaximizer & The Izotope Ozone 6 Maximizer. I found that the L3 Multimaxizer has the option to squeeze out loudness on certain frequency bands. Which makes it easy for you when you are comparing your mix to reference tracks.

For instance if you feel your reference track has a louder midrange then your track you just pull up some gain in the midrange to compensate with the reference. Very easy to use.

And with the Izotope maximizer I just got the feeling that I turned up the volume knob of that track. It sounded all very natural to me. It also had a neat feature to spare your transients which really made a difference in my track.

TIP 139

Do you master your mix differently for the Clubs vs Spotify & I-Tunes??

Nowadays we want the loudest possible master so that when your track is being played at the club it really pops out.

Now there are as many people agreeing as disagreeing on this subject.

But what happens if that same master is hitting the Radio or Spotify/ I-Tunes/ Youtube?

All those services use there own compression techniques. By that I mean the conversion to mp3, aac, ogg vorbis or whatever they use in combination with different bitrates and with different loudness standards.

For a club track I usually master somewhere between -6 / -3 LUFS on a drop. Which is pretty loud!

I've noticed that this is a very emotional subject. Some people would call you crazy if you master your track this loud. However this is still a loudness war. If the A&R of a recordcompany would listen to your track they will be definitely be influenced by this. Hate the game not the player.

Now I-Tunes streams at -16 LUFS
Youtube -13 LUFS and Spotify -12 LUFS.
Meaning that if you gave them your clubmaster they pull the volume of your track back to there loudness standard which could make your mix go from loud to sound soft & dull and less energetic.
Spotify does use limiting which could make it sound even more squashed.

So I recommend to use a plugin like 'Nugen Mastercheck' and create one master for the club and download portals and one more dynamic master for streaming services. However this is my personal opinion.

For Radio it's a different game. Every radiostation uses his own broadband compression techniques to put your music on the airwaves. If you would be interested in knowing how your track would sound on the biggest Hit Station of your country you could do the following.

You record a dance track you hear on your favorite hit station and then buy a WAV version of it as well. And start comparing and creating a broadcast compressor setting that comes close to the recorded radio track of your favorite radio station. I know people who actually have bought that broadcast compressor to make these kind of comparisons.But for the average joe this might not be interesting enough to pursue.

Fader Riding

If you recorded a very dynamic vocal. Meaning a big difference between the hardest and softest part of the acapella.

Then sometimes it's better to Fader ride that track instead of Hard compressing the vocal.

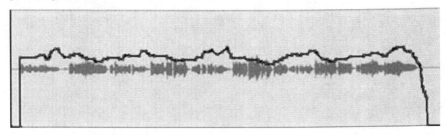

Or even better use a combination of slight compression and fader riding. Fader riding is when you manually draw in the volume on each vocal part.

That way you will even out the vocal way smoother without it sounding 'over-processed' and keeping it very natural.

It takes a bit longer, but it's worth it.

Distortion or Saturation?

What is the most important difference between Distortion or Saturation?

We could say that saturation is in fact also distortion. But saturation is mostly more subtle and intended to warm up a certain sound by adding extra related harmonic content which sound pleasing.

And Distortion is often used to alter your sound completely. Sometimes I take a regular bass patch and distort that into a snearping Lead sound.

But what most people don't realize is that saturation is a good way to create a very loud mix.
Because it decreases the dynamic range of a sound, cuts of the peaks somewhat and Pushes the sound more forward.
Which results in a pretty controlled volume of that track.

If you would apply the same technique to multiple stems you will get a more filled out frequency spectrum cause of all the added harmonic content which creates a louder mix.

TIP 142

Key Commands

Next to drag and drop, key commands are a producers wet dream.

It allows you to work faster, and in time you will control your DAW, like a secretary who is touch typing.

As far as I know every DAW has options to specify your keys. And even to put multiple actions underneath one Keystroke. These are called macros. It will cost you some time to create and master those but it will speedup your workflow to lightspeed.

And the great thing is that you can save your Key Commands and load them into another studio at a different location so you don't have to loose your workflow while working behind someone else his computer.

Studio One can even import key commands from multiple DAWS like cubase, logic and ProTools.

What's your favorite Key command?

How to stack musical layers on top of each other.

We have talked about layering before. But in that example we talked about layering synths that form one big sound.

We also talked about low-passing everything you don't need. For instance we discussed to NOT use the Solo button while cutting away the low end of a track. Cause this allows you to hear the direct effect of the low cut in your whole mix.

This is an alternative way, which is also very quick.

Let's say you have the Kick & the Bass.
On top of that you have some instruments. A Piano, Some strings and some Synth lines, like a Mid Lead and a High lead.

How do you go from there.
First decide which musical element has the lowest fundamentals.
If we look at our example it might be the following order

1. Piano
2. Mid-Lead
3. High Lead
4. Strings

In that case you would play the Kick and The Bass in a loop and start by putting the piano on top. Take a low cut filter and start cutting away the low end of the piano until you feel it still has low end but doesn't conflict or sounds thin. After that you mix in the Mid-Lead while playing the kick, bass & piano, and start cutting away the low end of this until you feel it still has low end but doesn't conflict with the other sounds (Piano, kick, bas) or sounds to thin. And so forth. This way you slide all elements together.

You could apply these techniques also on the stereo field for example.

Which of the 4 sounds do you want to sound the widest.
Rank them, and mix them like above. But in that case with panning and stereo widening techniques.

Marketing

If there isn't a market (yet), create one yourself.

If you produced a whole new genre which you are not sure people will understand immediately it always helps to create a few remixes / bootlegs in that same style as well.
The recognition of an already famous vocal makes you adapt easier to the instrumental underneath it.
If you release those tracks quickly after each other 3 to 4 weeks people will start to recognize your style even faster and you be sure to gain some traction.

TIP 145

Confidence

How to become more confident in releasing music instead of hoarding it. How to start overcoming your own perfectionism.

As a music producer you are probably never entirely happy with your song. And that's actually a good thing cause that is what makes you progress as a producer.
But how to decide when 'enough is enough'. To stop the tweaking and start releasing.
There are a few important Key factors to keep in mind here.

First off, The idea is more important then how it sounds. I usually take the song "Bromance by Avicii" as an example. This track works very well cause of the brilliant melodies and soundchoice. But from a mix perspective this song is really bad mixed. And I'm sure Tim realizes that as well.
In this case the mix is not inherent to the hit succes. And I can name a few more examples of tracks to where this applies to.
So If you made a melody that is stuck in your head forever you can be confident other people will going to like that too.

Second, there is also something like the festival experience. That track of which the drop sounds so fat over big sound systems that it doesn't really matter what the rest of the track does. It's all about that drop. Good example might be "Valentino Khan – Deep down Low".
If you hear that drop you immediately go bananas. But you can't really remember how the rest of the track goes.
So if you think you have a very strong drop, put a little more focus on that part of the song to make sure that is perfect and then you can be a little less critical on the rest of the song. Doesn't mean it should sound bad, but you can shift your focus a bit.

Third, Keep comparing your songs with other tracks that are already out there.
I don't mean comparing in the sense that you need to copy it.

But you already know how certain tracks sound in the club and or on the radio.

Always use those as references when mixing and arranging your tracks. Before sending your track to anyone (friends, labels, parents) make sure you at least come close to the soundquality you are referencing to.

Keep in mind that labels can scan a track in 5 seconds to determine if it's worth listening.

Finally, if you want to make Pop tracks like "Justin Bieber – Sorry" then you better make sure every second of your track is perfect ☺. Get some help from a mix engineer, a vocal engineer, a vocal coach, some text writers and some co-producers and a famous singer ;-)

The perfect intro in a dance music song

Making the intro part of a radio song. It seems like a very logical and easy thing to do. But it actually isn't.

You have 5 to 7 seconds to grab some ones attention to listen to your track. In that perspective "The Intro" becomes a super important part of your song to which you should pay special attention too.

How do you grab peoples attention in music. It's proven that people can only clearly distinct three elements in a track while listening to it. So if you could use the three best elements of your song which also clears the biggest part of your frequency range then that's what you should use. But make sure not to use more then three. And don't put your intro full of hard crashes and sweeps.

The most commonly used intro's excist of:

- Basline which plays along with the melody (low frequency spectrum)

- Chord stabs (could be guitar, piano, synths) (Low to Mid frequency spectrum)

- Catchy melody on top (could be the hookline) (Mid to High frequency spectrum)

- Something with a vocal. Could be a vocal effect an adlip or a real intro sung part. (Mid to High frequency spectrum)

It's important to create a 'warm' sounding intro that sounds inviting.

Now exceptions can easily be made on this rule. But only if one of these mentioned elements really stand out on their own.

NB: Intro's for video edits usually differ from radio versions.

TIP 147

When do I actually start using the compressor?

I always get a lot of questions about how to compress things. We already discussed quit a few things about it.

But when do you actually need to pull out the compressor in the first place?

When you are starting your mixdown, you are balancing your mix with your gain control plugins or/ and with your faders and by carving away some frequencies to give more room to specific instruments and boosting some frequencies to pull these sounds more upfront.

I personally don't use a lot of compression on individual tracks during my mixdown. When I do, it's mostly on the vocals which are always quit hard to balance well in your mix or certain transients which are just to present. Although I mostly use a transient designer for those peaks.

But there will always be elements in your mix that are hard to mix in. At some points in the track they would sound to hard and other points you can barely hear them. When you have that situation, you can decide to pull out the compressor or split the tracks in 2 and balance the specific parts seperately or use volume automation.

Since a compressor makes sure that the loudest peaks are getting softer and the softest peaks are getting louder you can create a steady volume level for your instrument which would be easier to balance in with the rest of your mix.

I mainly use compression only on group busses and the Final Mix bus. This is where they will make the biggest difference in your mix.

How to level the Sub Bas?

We discussed several things about how to balance the Kick vs Bass.
But how to determine how loud the subbas should be is really up to you
and the genre of music and the key that you are producing in.

The best answer I can give you is to load a few reference tracks in your
DAW and do the following:

SubBas are the frequencies below 60Hz. An to keep it simple we are going
to say they are between 32Hz and 60Hz.
You can open up your Fabfilter ProQ2 and set a point at +/- 46Hz. Add
a bit of Q, So that when we solo the frequency band it's roughly between
32 & 60 Hz.

Then open up a Spectrum Meter and put that one in One or Third Octave
mode so you get a clear view of the amount of Decibels per frequency and
use that as your mixing reference point for your subbas.

What is more important, good Speakers or a good acoustically treated room?

If your room is untreated you will have an uneven frequency response in your room. Which makes all your mixing decisions based on a sound that is 'coloured', because you can not accurately hear what is being played.

So if you step into your car to reference your freshly mixed track it will probably sound way different then you thought it would.

So making your room acoustically perfect is the most important thing you can do to your studio.

Now how to do that is a pretty complex study, which is very dependant on the sizes and materials of your room. Treating a room above 300Hz is easier then handling the lowend of a room (below 300Hz).

Below 300Hz is where you make a great difference for your studio.

Their are room ratio calculators which can help tell you at what roomsize the problem frequencies will be. You could look up the amroc calculator online.

They can give you as a layman some insights in where to place basstraps and the Subwoofer(s).

But getting the help of an acoustic specialist instead of buying that expensive pair of speakers is definitely the way to go.

What do I do will all these finished (ish) tracks?

I don't know if they're good enough. I don't know if or where to send for feedback I don't know if I should send it to labels or to DJ's or just put them on soundcloud for free.

So a couple of tips on this subject since I get a lot of those questions. If you are doubting if your track is good enough to send to a label then it probably isn't. The best way to go then is to reach the biggest audience you can possibly get for it.

So my suggestion would be the soundcloud(s) or facebook forums where you can post your stuff for feedback. I also roam some of these facebook forums and I'm sure other artist and labels do as well.

If your track IS good enough you will definitely get noticed and approached.

Or maybe release it yourself and invest some money in promoting it.

Sending your stuff to labels is something you should only do when you are 100% confident about the track.If you are new it might be best to start with some of the smaller labels. Although if you are confident enough you can start immediately with the big labels. But make sure your profile is present. Emailaddresses from A&R's usually trade hands via friends/ DJ's and management agencies. They are not publically posted for the simple reason that their mailbox would be flooded.
Getting feedback from well established producers is difficult.
In my case I get send a lot of stuff and I simply don't have the time to listen and give feedback on all of them. So I choose randomly as I'm sure my collegues do as well.

And finally when you have a lot of half-baked ideas it might be interesting to combine a few of those together to make one song.
This can create interesting combinations which also might lead to new genres.

TIP 151

FX Sends (AUX FX, Sends, FX buss)

This is a quick and simple tip which is much overlooked by producers.

If you use any effect via a send bus make sure you set the effect on 100% wet. This is not standard on most FX plugins when you open them.

Cause if you don't, and you mix in the effected signal on top of the Dry signal your sound will get louder since you are ALSO adding some of the unaffected signal back in your mix.

This can screw up your mix balance in a bad way.

TIP 152

Creating the perfect balance between Kick & Bass?

I know this is a question which people ask me a lot. And it always depends on the genre of music. However there is a way to create a perfect equal balance between Kick & Bass.

I saw this on Youtube the other day (source: Jacquire King) and wanted to apply it on EDM genres as well.

NB: I would only use this as a metering tool to find out if you have an equal balance between your kick and your bass. So try to see this technique seperate from how you are mixing all of your levels. It's especially usefull when you are mixing at a different environment.

And you can use it as a "Double check" for your ears, and only for the purpose of balancing your kick to your bass in a way where you would desire that. Depending on the genre you are making it sometimes makes sense to put the kick way harder then the bass or vica versa.

Having said that, check this out.

So you mix your kick like you would normally do. EQ, Compress, whatever. Same goes for your bassline(s). You mix those two towards each other, so you have some basis for the rest of your mix. You set your faders the way you want to as well.

After that to "double check" your balance you open up a VU-Meter. I'm using the one from Klanghelm.

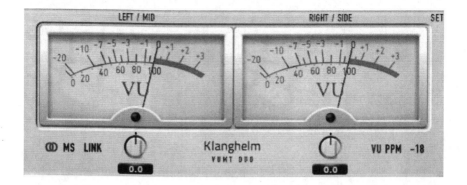

The theory behind it all is that if you have a Kick at -3dB RMS. And you'd copy that same kick underneath you will hit 0dB RMS. So on average you doubled the volume. Kick volume and bass volume is similar to each other. So if you can get the kick and the bass together hitting 0dB RMS you would have a perfect balance. - Jacquire King

Make sure you're kick is hitting -3dB on the VU, while using the gain knob on the VU plugin.

Then add the Bass to your mix and use the Volume FADER of the Bass to hit the 0dB on the VU Meter. After that Bypass the plugin and voila!

Stereo vs Mid-Side multiband compression

So today I want to point you in the right direction with a small assignment.

First a few terms:

- Stereo = 2 independent audio signals

- Mono = All audio signals mixed together and routed to one audio signal

- Side = is the difference between the left and right signal

- Mid = Everything that the left signal has in common with the right signal

Today I want to give you an assignment by taking your unmastered track and place 2 multiband compressors on your stereo bus. Pick one that has stereo and mid-side capabilities.

For instance in Izotope you can find one.

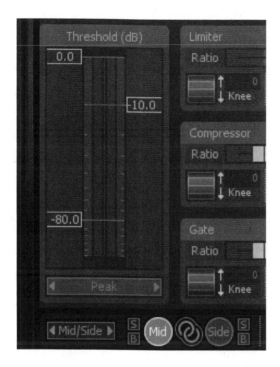

Now try to multiband compress your final mix in stereo mode to where you are happy with it. Then Mute it.

And then take the other multiband compressor and do the same thing but then in mid-side mode. Compress the mid information differently then the side information. For instance more compression on the mids then on the sides.

Now start A/B ing the two multiband compress settings and tell me which you find better sounding?

An interesting way of setting your levels.

At which levels do you start your mixdown? That's a question with one correct answer. And that is to leave some headroom left for the gain staging & mastering process. There are no correct numbers here.

Now everybody has different approaches on how to start their mixes. And even I differ in my methods from time to time just to experiment or to create a certain type of genre sound.

A great way to start your mixdown is by setting the level of the element you think should be the hardest in your mix or is the most important one of your mix. In dance music this is generally the Kick. But could also be the bass or vocal etc..

So you could start you mix by adjusting the level of your kick drum volume. You don't do this by pulling down the fader but by using a utility gain/ trim /channelstrip tool (depending on your daw). Meaning that you will have lowered the volume of the kick before it reaches the fader.

After that you start to make a rough mix of all the other elements around your kickdrum with the same technique. By using the gain/trim/channelstrip tool your DAW supplies. You could also try the Pink Noise trick here for creating a quick balance between all elements.

So the input balance of your mix is roughly made before you have even touched one fader.

After you have set the levels you can start EQ'ing, compressing and do all your magic.

With the faders this high it's much easier to make subtle volume changes then it would if you had pulled them down a lot in the beginning. This is because of the ratio's faders use. On the lower end it makes bigger dB steps then on the higher end of the fader.

A logical step after this is to group the same frequency elements to group busses and add some additional gain staging before slamming a master compressor on the masterchannel

The Pink Noise Trick

The human hearing system's frequency range response is not linear but logarithmic.
White noise has constant energy across the frequency spectrum, and Pink noise contains the same amount of energy per octave. Creating a naturally balanced sound for the human ear.
Pink noise could help you quickly set a balance between all your elements.

Now how does this work. You take a noise generator or a pink noise audio sample (copy that to the length of your track). Calibrate the pink noise so that, at the stereo bus, it registers an average level for mixing on your meters.
Then solo the first element of your mix so that it plays alongside the pink noise and start balancing it against the Pink noise. You are aiming for that point where you can just hear it above the noise. For the balancing try the trick of tip 154 instead of using the faders.

Now start doing this for all your tracks. One by one until you have had them all. Then delete the Pink noise and what should be left is a great starting point of a balanced mix. From here on out you can start balancing further with your faders, applying eq's, compressors etc..
Since we are making dance music the kick and bass can be set a bit higher in general.

Ooh btw it also helps to calm your baby down. But that's a different blog.